The Life of Malcolm X

The Life of
MALCOLM X
by Richard Curtis

Macrae Smith Company

PHILADELPHIA

Copyright © 1971 by Richard Curtis
Library of Congress Catalog Card Number 70-150675
Manufactured in the United States of America
Published simultaneously in Canada
by George J. McLeod, Limited, Toronto
SBN: 8255-2786-4

Book design by Adrianne Dudden
7105

To my friend
JEFF BERGSTEIN (1944–1970)
for the pleasure of his company

Acknowledgment

My deepest thanks to Dave Fisher, whose contribution to this book can never be sufficiently acknowledged

Contents

The Life of Malcolm X

one | *The Man and His Movement*

SUNDAY, February 21, 1965, was the first day of National Brotherhood Week. In New York City's Washington Heights section a crowd of 400 people, almost all of them black, had gathered at the Audubon Ballroom to hear black militant speaker Malcolm X. The meeting had been called by Malcolm in an attempt to recruit members for his newly founded movement called the Organization of Afro-American Unity. While Malcolm, who had been late himself after stopping at a nearby restaurant for a banana split and a cup of tea, sat backstage waiting for the other scheduled speaker to appear, Brother Benjamin X spoke to the audience. After almost an hour had passed, it became obvious that the man Malcolm was waiting for was not going to show up, so Brother Benjamin finished his speech.

"And now," he told the audience, "I present to you one who is willing to put his life on the line for you. A man who would give his life for you. One who is a trojan for the black man, Brother Malcolm X." In just a few moments Benjamin X was to find out just how true his words were.

The curtain behind the introductory speaker parted and Malcolm X, with a small smile on his lips, walked forward to the speaker's stand. He paused and looked over the audience, then he gave the traditional Arabic greeting, "Asalaikum," meaning *peace be with you*.

Many people in the audience answered, "Asalaikum salaam," *peace be with you, brother*.

The ballroom was totally silent as the audience waited for Malcolm to begin. Then, just as he started to speak, two men sitting in a middle row began fighting. "Take your hand out of my pocket," an angry voice shouted. Everyone in the room turned to see what the noise was all about. Malcolm's bodyguards reacted quickly and began running toward the men.

"Hold it! Hold it!" Malcolm said, raising his hand and stepping from behind the rostrum, "Let's cool it, brothers—" They were the last words he would ever speak.

From the area left vacant by the bodyguards a Negro, later identified as a member of the Black Muslim movement, approached the stage. Taking a sawed-off shotgun from beneath his coat, he took careful aim and fired point blank at the startled Malcolm X. His hand still raised in the air in a gesture of peace, Malcolm's body began falling straight backward. The two men who had started the fight drew revolvers of their own and began firing into the body of the fallen leader. In an instant it was over. Malcolm's wife ran to the stage screaming, "My husband, they're killing my husband," but by the time she reached him it was too late. Sixteen shells had entered his body and Malcolm X, who had been born in poverty 39 years earlier and risen to become one of the most powerful black leaders in American history, was dead.

News of the assassination spread quickly across the nation. Most television stations broke into their regularly scheduled programs with news of the shooting, much to the displeasure of a nationally published newspaper columnist who didn't understand why it was necessary to interrupt a performance of the ballet *Swan Lake*. Many newspapers rushed extra editions onto the streets, and they all told the same story on page one: the story of a black boy born into poverty who had dropped out of school in eighth grade and turned to a life of crime and dependence on narcotics.

He had been arrested for robbery at age 19 and given a ten-year sentence. While in prison he discovered a man named Elijah Muhammad, who headed a small, all-black religious group known as the Muslims. After educating himself in prison, the newspaper stories continued, he was paroled and under Muhammad's guidance soon became a Muslim Minister. He preached that black and white men could never be brothers, that instead of expecting peace and love from whites, the Negro should expect violence and hatred. His bitter and violent speeches had helped the Muslim movement grow from 400 to an estimated 40,000.

But in the last two years of his life, because of a conflict with Elijah Muhammad, he had left the Muslims. After two trips to Africa he had started preaching a different message—that men of all colors could indeed live together in true brotherhood. He admitted that he had made many mistakes as a Muslim and began openly to criticize Muhammad and his movement. In fact, most newspapers concluded that it was this change in attitude that had provoked Malcolm X's murder by members of the Black Muslims.

Malcolm's followers seemed to agree. The night after the shooting, the four-story building in New York City's Harlem ghetto that housed Black Muslim Temple #7 was burned to the ground. Just eleven years earlier Malcolm had been sent from Boston by Muhammad to take charge of the rented storefront that then served as the New York meeting place. In the decade that followed, because of his dynamic speaking ability and his militant views on black-white relations, he became the spokesman for a great number of American blacks and thus one of the most controversial figures in the nation. In 1964 American college students voted him the second most popular campus speaker. The only man ahead of him was Senator Barry Goldwater, the Republican nominee for the Presidency of the United States that year.

And now Malcolm X was dead, the victim of the very movement he had helped to reach national status, the victim of the very feelings he had aroused. Yet in death as in life he remained a man both deeply loved and deeply hated.

"I knew him as a wonderful man," said a Negro workingman, one of the 22,000 blacks and whites who walked by his open coffin to pay their final respects, "a great man, a prince of peace, a nobleman."

"All he ever did was talk," said a black housewife. "While all those other groups were out there doin', he was talkin', that's all, just talkin'."

Famed black writer James Baldwin called Malcolm's death "a major setback for the Negro movement." The weekly newsmagazine *Time* disagreed, saying, "Malcolm X in life and in death was a disaster to the civil rights movement."

The division of opinion was no more evident than in the well-respected newspaper *The New York Times*. While on page one the *Times* referred to Malcolm as "a bearded extremist," a story inside told of a Negro youth who announced he wanted to die beside Malcolm's coffin and then challenged a policeman to shoot him.

Whether they loved him or hated him, no one could deny his importance. He was the first to offer an alternative to the nonviolent path the civil rights movement had been following, and all blacks, militant or nonviolent, gained from his presence on the scene. James Hicks, editor of the Harlem newspaper *The Amsterdam News,* explained how important Malcolm X had been to the nonviolent leaders. "These leaders would go to the whites," Hicks said, "and say to them, 'You've got to deal with us or with people like Malcolm!' " Either way it was a victory for black people.

The controversy quieted, at least for one day, Saturday, February 27. Early in the afternoon the man who had been born Malcolm Little and known at different times as "Satan," "Big Red," and "Detroit Red" and had gained worldwide attention as Malcolm X was buried in a New York cemetery under his Moslem name, El-Hajj Malik El-Shabazz. But as far as the movement for black equality in the United States was concerned, the end of

Malcolm's life marked the beginning of an entirely new era.

Malcolm remains as important in death as he was in life. A female social worker in the Los Angeles black ghetto, Watts, best described the ever-present influence of Malcolm X: "There's a great hang-up among black youth today. Everything you propose to these kids is measured and carefully thought out. They try to figure out whether Malcolm would approve or not."

Because Malcolm-in-memory has become an important factor in the new, more militant civil rights movement, the questiton of "whether Malcolm would approve or not" is a very important one, and one to which no one exactly knows the answer. At the time of his death Malcolm was in the process of changing his whole attitude toward white people. The things he saw on his trips to Africa changed many of his opinions. Where he had once been totally against any contact between blacks and whites, he had come to the point where he could understand marriage between members of the two races. Where he had once demanded that land be given to American blacks in payment for their years of slavery, he began urging all Negroes to take part in the democratic process —to get out and vote. And while he once had only spoken of whites as "devils," he had begun speaking of them as brothers. No wonder there is confusion as to "whether Malcolm would approve or not."

No one has yet satisfactorily answered the question Who was Malcolm X and what did he stand for? Above all, he stood for black pride, but he stood for much more than just that. To understand exactly what he stood for to the black American it is necessary to know what were the major influences of his life.

Although slavery had legally ended in America with adoption of the Thirteenth Amendment to the Constitution just after the Civil War, the South continued to keep its black citizens in chains by adopting a series of unwritten laws called "Black Codes." These "codes," which were enforced by violence, fear and trickery, enabled the South and many areas of the North to continue to deprive the Negro of his constitutional rights. In the fifty years following the Civil War the black man was almost totally eliminated from American society.

In 1896 this "separate society" was ruled legal by the Supreme Court. A New Orleans Negro named Homer Plessy tried to ride in a "white only" railroad coach. He was arrested and then convicted of breaking a "whites only" law. The case went all the way to the Supreme Court, and the high court said there was nothing wrong with keeping blacks and whites separate "as long as the state provided equal facilities."

Immediately, separate (white only) schools were founded, and separate restaurants, hotels, washrooms— even water fountains—popped up. And while certainly separate, they were rarely equal. Although the black man had his freedom, that was all he had. Equal opportunity for advancement was denied him. The right to work wherever he wanted was denied. The right to vote in elections, the right to use public transportation, and even the right to live wherever he wanted, all basic rights under the Constitution, were denied the Negro. Times had not really changed much from the days of slavery. The black man was still, in every way possible, a second-class citizen.

Into this atmosphere came two men who were to serve as primary examples to Malcolm and the entire black militant movement, two men who refused to accept the punishment that went with the crime of being born black in America, W. E. DuBois and Marcus Garvey.

DuBois was born in 1868 and at age 27 became the first black man to obtain his doctoral degree from Harvard University. Through the Niagara Movement, which he founded in 1905, and a magazine called *The Horizon,* which he started editing in 1907, he demanded full and equal rights for black citizens.

DuBois felt it was the duty of those few Negroes who had been relatively successful to lead the fight for all Negroes. For this reason he was a harsh critic of what today are called "Uncle Toms"—black men who act in every way as if they were white. His favorite target was scientist-educator Booker T. Washington, whom he accused of hurting the black cause by not speaking out against the white man. Malcolm X would follow DuBois' example and criticize Dr. Martin Luther King for his nonviolent strategy.

Before his death in the African nation of Ghana in 1963 at the age of ninety-five, DuBois had become deeply involved in the struggle for world peace and been an early leader of the movement to ban atomic weapons. Unfortunately, because he had become a member of the Communist Party, many of his important contributions to the civil rights movement have been overlooked.

Marcus Garvey had a more direct and more important influence on the life of Malcolm X. Garvey was born in the West Indies in 1887 and came to America to promote a single idea: "uniting all the Negro peoples of the world into one great body and establishing a country and a government absolutely their own."

The Garvey nation was to be founded somewhere

in Africa—an idea that Malcolm X was to promote in the future. Two-term President James Madison had promoted it in the past. (In 1819 Madison said, "To be consistent with existing . . . prejudices in the United States the freed blacks ought to be permanently removed beyond the region occupied by . . . a white population." Later he added, "If an asylum could be found in Africa, that would be an appropriate destination for the unhappy race among us.")

Garvey was one of the first blacks to try to turn the thought into reality. He founded an organization that he called the United Negro Improvement Association. The UNIA existed to fulfill two goals: freedom for the nations in Africa that had been conquered by white countries, and the establishment of the black nation.

Garvey also founded *Negro World,* the most widely read black newspaper of the early 1900's. This was another example that Malcolm carefully followed. In order to help recruit new members of the Muslim movement he founded a newspaper called *Muhammad Speaks.*

Marcus Garvey was indeed a man Malcolm X patterned himself after, intentionally or not. "Prayer alone is not going to improve our conditions," Garvey told his followers, "nor can the policy of watchful waiting." One of the last things Malcolm told the people who believed in him was, "I believe in action, period. Whatever kind of action is necessary."

Although Garvey had founded the UNIA in Kingston, Jamaica, it had a small membership until he settled in Harlem in the early 1900's. By the time the "Roaring Twenties" began there were over 30 branches in the United States, and many more rural preachers were echoing his militant ideas. One of them was a tall, dark-

skinned midwestern Baptist Minister, the Reverend Earl
Little, Malcolm's father.

Reverend Little was a wandering preacher, never
having a pulpit of his own but usually staying in one
place long enough to gain many black supporters—and
white enemies. After settling for a time in Philadelphia
and Milwaukee, he moved to Omaha, Nebraska. It was
in Omaha that Malcolm, the fourth child of his marriage
to Louise Little, was born. The preacher had three other
children by a first marriage.

Earl Little was known in the language of the day
as a "jock-leg" preacher, meaning that he was as much
a politician as a religious leader. His politics were those
handed down by Marcus Garvey, and they all centered
around the same idea—pride in the individual. Earl
Little felt that the black man could never really be free
in a country he came to in chains. And since that meant
that the Negro could never gain his freedom and dignity
in America, the only course open to him was to return
to Africa. Reverend Little urged his followers to forget
white Gods, to reject white society, and to free themselves of their American-made chains.

He did this at a time in American history when it
was very dangerous for a black man to speak out, and
the Little family suffered for it. While Louise Little was
pregnant with the future Malcolm X, a group of white
citizens from Omaha, covering their faces and bodies
with white sheets, the symbol of a terrorist group still
existing today known as the Ku Klux Klan, smashed all
the windows of the Little home with the butts of their
rifles. Only the fact that Earl Little was away preaching
kept him from being attacked. Realizing that it was only
a matter of time before the Klan returned, Earl Little

moved his family to Lansing, Michigan, as soon as Malcolm was born.

In Lansing the terrorist group was known as the Black Legion, but their tactics were the same. Young Malcolm's very first memory was of being awakened in the middle of the night and having to flee for his life from his burning home. Two white men, deciding to get even with Reverend Little for spreading the Garvey way of thinking, had set fire to his house. It burned to the ground. But Earl Little was not one to give up. His determination was another trait Malcolm would inherit.

The preacher had been raised in a violent atmosphere. Four of his five brothers had met violent deaths, and somewhere he himself had had an eye poked out. He was not going to let something as simple as a fire scare him off. This was a lesson Malcolm was to remember years later when his own Long Island home was set afire. Earl Little's answer to those who tried to scare him off was to move his family within the East Lansing city limits and build a second home. This was the house in which Malcolm spent his early years.

The thing Malcolm was to remember best about his father was his strong sense of discipline. "There is a right way and there is a wrong way," he told his children, "and you will always do things the right way!" The penalty for the slightest mistake was a severe beating. But for some reason the only child Earl Little never hit was Malcolm. Although Malcolm never understood why he escaped with nothing more than lectures while his brothers and sisters were given good whippings, he guessed it had something to do with the color of his skin. In those days the shade of a Negro's skin was very important. Since most black parents felt their lighter-skinned children stood a much better chance for success in the white world, these children were usually treated much better than their darker brothers and sisters.

Malcolm never had a chance to ask his father about this. One sunny afternoon Earl Little's enemies finally caught up with him and he was found laid out across the local streetcar tracks, the side of his head bashed in.

Louise Little was almost the exact opposite of her husband. While he was extremely dark in color with a thick, broad nose, she was almost white. While Earl Little spoke in a pronounced Negro dialect, Louise Little sounded just like a white woman. Malcolm and his brothers and sisters were well aware of the difference and the reasons for it. Louise's mother, Malcolm's grand-mother, had been forced to have sexual relations with a white man—a relationship that produced the half-white, half-black baby girl who was named Louise. It was her white blood and skin color that Malcolm inherited.

Although he grew to be 6 feet 3 inches tall, just an inch less than his father, Malcolm most resembled his mother. In addition to his light skin color, his hair had a reddish tint to it. His facial features were a delicate mixture of Negro and Caucasian. His mother was well aware that Malcolm was most like her, and if that saved him from his father's anger it had just the opposite effect where Louise was involved. She was well aware that a complexion as light as his put him in a racial no-man's land—he would fit in neither the black world nor the white world—and she tried to prepare him for this.

"Go out and get some sun," she would tell him, "so you can get some color." She made it a point never to let him feel superior to any of his brothers or sisters. And when he had done something for which she felt he deserved to be punished, she was the one who did the whipping, even over her husband's objections. But above everything else, as Earl Little had given Malcolm pride, Louise Little gave him a love for learning, a thirst for education.

The year 1925, when Malcolm was born, saw a number of landmarks in race relations. Marcus Garvey, in jail for stock fraud, lost his appeal for a second trial and was sent back to prison. A black student was admitted to the American Government's School of Diplomacy and, when the other students refused to go to class with him, was graduated without being required to attend any classes. And a report issued by all-black Tuskegee Institute said that only 16 black persons had been killed as the result of mob violence. This figure included lynchings and burnings at the stake. What it didn't include was disappearances and "accidents" of the type Earl Little was soon to suffer. As young Malcolm was soon to find out, things were to get worse, not better.

two | *Growing Up*

T HE grassy rise out behind the Littles' house in Lansing was known as Hector's Hill, and it seemed to have been made just so boys could lie there on lazy summer days and watch the billowing white puffs slowly float by. Malcolm spent many of his childhood hours on Hector's Hill watching those clouds of July and August and dreaming the dreams of all young boys. But there was no chance Malcolm's dreams would ever come true —America's depression and his father's death would see to that.

The nation was thrown into an economic shock on a bright October day in 1929. Millions of people had invested in the stock market using the credit system, "Buy now, pay later!" For many reasons a financial panic began and the bankers began demanding immediate payments. It was impossible for most people to make these payments, and thus millions lost all the money they had.

Within weeks, banks had closed their doors all over the nation, never to reopen. More important, the long lines that were representative of this period began forming outside the state-run welfare offices. The routine inside these offices was simple: the person signing up for welfare would fill in a few forms, undergo investigation by a welfare worker, and receive the basic necessities for survival.

The "Great Crash" didn't affect the Little family, at least not immediately. When you haven't very much there isn't very much you can lose. And the things Malcolm had—a father he greatly admired, a mother who took care of him and worried about him, two big brothers and a big sister to look up to, as well as a little brother who looked up to him—these were things that money couldn't buy.

The necessities were easily taken care of. Clothes could be made, and were. The four-room house Earl Little had built just a few years ago was still warm and sturdy, and the family had long depended on nature to provide food. Although Louise Little hated to cook rabbits, the woods were full of them and Malcolm became an excellent shot at an early age. Earl Little had long ago started raising chickens, which provided tasty meals. And there was always more land to enlarge the family garden. Very early in his life Malcolm's parents taught him to depend on "the gifts of God," and the pride and joy of his early years was his own little vegetable garden.

But all of this began to change the day Earl Little went into town and was caught by his enemies. Malcolm was just six years old when his mother told him he would never see his father alive again.

Death was still too large an idea for Malcolm to understand. All he knew was that three days before, his father had been teaching him how to weed his garden, and now he was lying still in a plain wooden box.

Malcolm walked slowly up to his father's coffin and stared down at the man who had meant so much to him. Instead of sorrow he felt hollow inside. The ashen-white color of his father's skin both disgusted and fascinated him. And as was the custom among black families, the Little house was so filled with family friends that for Malcolm the funeral actually became fun. Death did not seem so very unbearable to him. Then the visitors stopped coming, and he became aware of the terrible emptiness inside the house.

But it would still be many months before the family would feel the full force of Earl Little's death. Because he was aware that death was never far away, Malcolm's father had taken out two life insurance policies, and although one of the companies refused to pay off, the family managed to survive on the payment from the second.

In order to help make ends meet, Malcolm's oldest brother, Wilfred, dropped out of school and began taking odd jobs. Louise Little entrusted the care of Malcolm and his younger brother to the older sister and went into Lansing to look for a job. Because she could pass for white she had no trouble finding one, but as soon as Malcolm and his darker-colored brothers showed up she would be fired. She would then find another job until the same thing happened.

The other children all pitched in to help in whatever ways they could. And so for a while things went along quite smoothly. It seemed that the Little family was managing to recover from the loss of the head of the household. They began to settle into a routine, living together, laughing together and working together. Then the "Great Depression" reached the Midwest.

A depression is like an upside-down pyramid. It starts from a small base and gradually gets bigger and bigger. For Malcolm the depression came to Lansing in many different ways. When the final chicken was eaten there was no more money to buy another one; vegetable plants became a luxury; there was no thought of any new clothes. When something broke, it was repaired if at all possible, because there was no money to replace it.

But Louise and Wilfred continued to find work in Lansing, so there was always some food on the table. Since flour was the cheapest of all basic foods Malcolm and one of his brothers would be sent into town to buy a big bag, and Louise would turn the flour into hundreds of different dishes. Malcolm had never realized how many different kinds of food and gravy could be made from flour. Every once in a while, though, there wasn't even enough money to buy the flour bag, and on those occasions a big pot of dandelion greens would serve as dinner. These were the hardest days of Malcolm's young life, and he would never forget what living in poverty was like.

One afternoon when Malcolm was in Lansing buying flour he saw a long line outside a small store. Each person in the line would go into the store and come out

carrying a big bag of flour and some other food pack-
ages. When he found out the food was being given away
free he ran home to tell his mother of his wonderful
discovery. Instead of putting on her coat and going right
into town as Malcolm thought she would, Louise Little
became very quiet.

"I know all about the free food," she said, "and it
isn't really free."

Malcolm didn't understand. All he saw was a long
line of people getting food and not paying for it. What
he didn't know was that the family had to give up all
their privacy in order to get that "free" food. They had
to let the state welfare workers come in and take over
their lives. The legacy of pride and independence that
Earl Little had left to his family made it impossible for
Louise to accept this charity.

But eventually pride will give way to hunger, and
independence to survival. When jobs became harder to
get, there was very little food on the table. Malnutrition
was a serious problem in the household now, and the
Little family had no choice but to accept the state aid.
More important, with this physical deterioration came a
loss of the spirit that had kept the family together during
the past year. These were blows from which Malcolm's
mother would never really recover.

"It seemed," Malcolm once remembered, "that everything in our house was stamped 'Not to Be Sold.' All
welfare food bore this stamp to keep the people who
received it from selling it. It's a wonder that we didn't
come to think of 'Not to Be Sold' as a brand name."

Although the family was now eating regularly,
Louise Little's worst fears came true. With the welfare
food came the welfare workers. After a few weeks of

poking around the house they began talking about taking the younger children away from Louise and placing them with other families in town. "Wouldn't you like your children to have new clothes and adult supervision all day?" they would ask Louise.

With great anger she would answer, "But you can't give them their own flesh and blood that loves them."

In the end, though, there was no question about who would win. Louise Little was working day and night at any job she could find and was still having great trouble making ends meet. Because she could not be home as often as she liked she was constantly worrying about her children. To add to everything else, she was trying to maintain her own personal life and had finally met a man she really liked. The strain was slowly proving too much for her to handle. Instead of helping out, Malcolm was just causing more problems.

As he grew up, Malcolm graduated from the boyhood games of taking vegetables from a neighbor's garden to stealing fruit from produce stands in Lansing. He began taking everything he could get his hands on, although food was usually his target. Naturally this focused the attention of the welfare people on him. They made it seem that everything he did was a major crime.

For example, one afternoon he worked in a strawberry patch and made almost a dollar. On his way into Lansing he met a white schoolmate of his who taught him the game of flipping coins. They would both throw a coin into the air and Malcolm would call out either heads or tails. If both coins came up the way he called, then he would win them both. If they did not, he would lose. Within a few moments Malcolm had lost all his money but learned an important lesson about gambling.

The welfare people treated the event as a major fall. They were convinced that he was about to become a gambler and was well on his way to a life of crime. The only solution, they felt, was separating the family. And finally they won. Louise Little, slowly losing the ability to resist, agreed to let Malcolm live with another family.

Actually, the welfare people did not move Malcolm very far; just across town to the home of the Gohannas family. Although his mother had agreed to the separation, his departure dealt a bitter blow. Within a few months she suffered a nervous breakdown and had to be put in the state mental hospital. Her condition did not improve in the hospital. She kept slipping further and further from reality until she didn't even recognize Malcolm when he came for his weekly visit. Embittered, Malcolm swore he would never forget how the state had broken up his family. What's more, he was convinced it was the actions of the welfare people, all of them white, that had caused his mother to become sick.

Not that life with the Gohannas family was all that bad. They had a nephew about Malcolm's age living with them at the time and the two boys got along very well. For Malcolm life became a series of weekend rabbit hunts, children's games, Halloween pranks and, of course, school and homework. But the games they were playing changed in 1937 when a Negro boxer named Joe Louis defeated James J. Braddock and became heavyweight champion of the world. "The Brown Bomber," as Louis was known, became the first real idol black youngsters had ever had, and interest in boxing surpassed everything else. Malcolm was no different from thousands of other boys his age: he decided that someday he too would be the champ!

Because he looked much older than his 13 years he had no trouble getting his first amateur fight. Winning it was something else. He knew absolutely nothing about boxing and although he was a pretty good allround athlete, he didn't stand much chance against his first, more experienced opponent. Malcolm decided that the best thing to do would be to come out swinging in the first round and try to knock his opponent out. So he trained for a short fight.

It didn't turn out quite the way he expected. "I knew when I came out of my corner that I was scared, but I didn't know, as my opponent told me later, that he was scared of me too. He was so scared he knocked me down fifty times if he did it once." Malcolm was tired after the first round. After the second round he was almost exhausted. He could hardly get off the stool for the third round and lost the fight. But he had learned two important lessons: never underestimate your opponent, and always train for the long battle, even if you think you can win the short one.

And that is exactly what he did when he heard that he was scheduled for a rematch. He trained long and hard for the second fight, but of course the scene was different. This time his opponent knocked him down with his first punch, and by the time Malcolm woke up they were almost ready to start the next fight. "I knew then that I was never going to be champion." Malcolm joked about his short, unsuccessful ring career.

Unfortunately, those were not the only fights Malcolm got into—but they were the only ones that took place in the boxing ring. Although he certainly was not the neighborhood terror, he started to get into more and more trouble. Finally he pulled one prank too many and was expelled from school for bad conduct. The courts arranged to have him sent to a reform school, but while the paperwork was being prepared he was sent to live in a detention home. There he met Mr. and Mrs. Swerlin, the white couple who ran the home.

Mrs. Swerlin was a roly-poly woman with a glint in her eye and a smile on her face. She looked as though she belonged over a pot of delicious food all the time. Her husband was just the opposite, small and serious. Both of them liked Malcolm immediately and he responded to them. A mutual admiration between Malcolm and the Swerlins developed. They exercised complete control over all the boys, both black and white, who stayed with them. But they also did their best to encourage individuality. They promoted friendships, treated each child equally, and always made sure the work load was evenly divided. For the first time in his life Malcolm had a room of his own. Often he would close the door and just lie still on his bed, trying to get used to the idea of privacy. More important, he had good food every day, clean clothes, and an understanding woman to listen to his problems.

Malcolm was enrolled in the Mason Junior High School. There was only one other black in the entire school. After brushing up on the material he had missed, Malcolm went right to the head of his class. The Swerlins even got him a job washing dishes in a restaurant so he could have some pocket money of his own, and no one said a word when he went home each weekend to see his brothers and sisters. He was as proud as he could be when he took some pennies out of his pocket and gave them to his younger brother to buy some candy.

His life outside the classroom was good too. Although his social life was limited because there were no black girls in the school, he got along well with all the other students. He was a member of the basketball team and just about every club in the junior high. He was a top debater and learned to love defeating people with words instead of fists. But his proudest moment came when his classmates elected him president of their class. It was later that Malcolm was to come to believe that his popularity was due to his uniqueness as one of only two black persons in the school. He was the Mason Junior High Negro. Had there been more blacks in the school, Malcolm was soon to believe, he would have been treated far differently.

On the outside, Malcolm was always smiling and laughing. It was deep inside that racial problems were beginning to bother him. People had called him names like "Nigger" and "Rastus" so often when he was younger that he had never even realized they were insults. Even the Swerlins had used words like that in his presence, but now, for the first time, they were beginning to disturb him.

And he began to notice that there were real differences between people with black skin and people with white skin. White people, he thought, smelled differently from blacks. And eating with the Swerlins and the other occupants of the detention house had convinced him that white people liked different foods from blacks, and liked their food prepared quite differently from the way his mother had prepared it for the family.

Most important, he began to realize that the other students in his class were well aware of the difference in color. When he was alone with a bunch of boys he was treated no differently from anyone else, but the picture changed when a girl was involved. If a white girl came around, the others seemed to pretend that Malcolm did not even exist. They would never bother to introduce him to the girl or invite him along when the boys and girls went somewhere together. These new racial feelings were something Malcolm had never encountered, and he wasn't sure how to deal with them. It would take him many years, but he would learn.

To complicate these new feelings, Malcolm was just beginning to get interested in girls. He knew he was supposed to stay in the background when white girls were present, but he still managed to develop friendships with some of the Mason Junior High girls. Because he knew he would never be dating any of them his manner was free, easy, and calm, and many of the girls were attracted to him. Because he didn't seem to pay any attention to them, as he had been taught, the girls would go out of their way to attract his attention.

Of course the situation was exactly reversed when he would go into Lansing to meet some Negro girls. He would go to a dance and become so tense and nervous that he would stand in a corner and never dare venture out onto the dance floor. Although he often wanted to start a conversation, he never could figure out exactly what to say. Malcolm had indeed changed since being separated from his family: he now felt right at home with white people and was lost with members of his own race. Through the Swerlins, through school and through his job, Malcolm was becoming more and more "whitewashed" everyday. He was well on his way to becoming the "house-nigger."

The "cultural shock" that Malcolm needed to remind him that he was still a black man in a white society came in the person of his half-sister Ella. She was one of Earl Little's three children by a previous marriage and had gone to Boston years ago to make her fortune. She had indeed been successful. She had married a doctor, and even though she had divorced him she was now considered an important member of Boston's black community. She had taken it upon herself to watch out for and protect her brothers and sisters. "We Littles got to stick together," she would shout at Malcolm in her booming voice, "'cause we're all we got."

Although Malcolm had never met Ella, he had been writing to her in Boston since his arrival at the Swerlins'. One day he received the answer he had been hoping to get: Ella was coming to Lansing to meet her family. The very next day she arrived. Ella burst into Lansing like a hurricane. Malcolm loved her at first sight.

Ella immediately took charge of putting the family back together again. One day she would take them all to visit Louise Little in the state hospital. The next day she would take Malcolm out all alone and spend hours telling him about members of the family he had never met. And meals with Ella were not as much a chance to eat as an opportunity for the children to hear about the wondrous city of Boston. "She was," Malcolm remembered, "the first really proud black woman I had ever met. I was totally overwhelmed by her." It was an impression he was not soon to forget.

Just before she left Lansing, Ella invited Malcolm to spend the coming summer with her. It was all Malcolm could do to keep from getting on the bus with her right then and there! School couldn't end soon enough, even for the class President. Finally, with his report card in hand so he could show Ella just how smart the Little family was, he boarded the cross-country bus and headed East. He was leaving the land he had grown up on, the land he knew intimately, for the first time. For all practical purposes he would never come home again.

Boston. The Hub. Beantown. Neon lights, nightclubs, blaring music, fancy clothes, huge stores, soda fountains on every corner. An entire new world was opening to Malcolm—and he just stood at the bus terminal with his mouth hanging wide open. In his wildest dreams he had never imagined anything as beautiful yet as strange as Boston. He compared the ill-fitting nonmatching clothes he had on to those worn by the people who walked by him, and he almost turned right then and got back on the first bus home. But as usual Ella came to the rescue. "A lot of people have arrived here better dressed than you," she told him, "but you got something going for you they don't have—a good, bright mind. Make sure you use it. Now let's go home."

Ella was living with her second husband, a soldier, in the Sugar Hill section of Boston's Negro ghetto, Roxbury. After Malcolm had calmed down a little, Ella told him all the important things he would have to know: where the bus lines were, how to use the subways, places to stay out of and places to go into. Then she let him go out and wander on his own.

Malcolm's first impression of Boston was that he was in a black wonderland. There were more black people in Roxbury than Malcolm had ever realized existed in the whole world. An entire social structure of black people. Black doctors, bus drivers, soda jerks, and shoe salesmen. Rich blacks and poor blacks. The existence of a black society was something Malcolm had never even thought about, and now here it was, right in front of him.

Boston was totally indescribable for Malcolm. He spent the summer meeting new and different types of people, exploring every stoop and alley of Roxbury, and seeing some of the famous places he had seen pictures of in his history books.

One day Ella took him on one of their periodic trips to downtown Boston. "This is where the Revolutionary War started, Malcolm," she told him. "A group of British soldiers fired on an unarmed crowd and killed one of them. His name was Crispus Attucks and he was a black man. He was the first American to die in defense of this country. And one more thing you should remember, Malcolm: Crispus Attucks was a slave." Malcolm was totally amazed to learn that fact, and when he started thinking about it, he wondered why none of his history books ever mentioned any black heroes.

The summer seemed to fly by. Before he knew it it was time for Malcolm to return to the Swerlins'. But as his bus pulled out of Boston, Malcolm made a promise to himself that he would be back many, many times.

Life back at the Swerlins' was not as easy as it had been. Living in a totally black society for the first time had magnified those small black-white differences he had first started noticing just before he left. Now he began to feel very uncomfortable when he was around white people. He became more and more withdrawn. He began spending many hours behind the closed door of his room, looking for his own answers to the things that were bothering him, rather than discussing them with white people.

The change in Malcolm was very evident to those around him. The very classmates who had elected him President the year before now began to shy away. Although he himself didn't know the reason for his dissatisfaction he knew he was terribly unhappy—and extremely restless. The Swerlins noticed all that was happening and tried to persuade Malcolm to confide in them, but it did no good. How could he tell them about the new world he had discovered? How could he explain it to them when he didn't really understand it himself? He elected to say nothing. Malcolm needed his own people.

His new realizations were dramatized one afternoon when he stayed after class to discuss a future project with his favorite teacher, Mr. Ostrowski, who taught English. That afternoon Malcolm's class had been discussing how to succeed in the world and how much could be accomplished by hard work and honesty. So it was the most natural thing in the world for Mr. Ostrowski to take this after-hours opportunity to ask Malcolm about his future. "Just what do you think you'd like to do when you get a little older, Malcolm?" he asked.

Up until that moment Malcolm had never given his future a thought; he was having enough trouble understanding his newly discovered racial awareness. So he said the very first thing that came to his mind. "I think I'd like to be a lawyer." There was a long silence as Mr. Ostrowski considered exactly what to say. Malcolm expected to hear the encouraging remarks that were part of everyday classroom language. He was amazed at his teacher's answer.

"Malcolm," Mr. Ostrowski said, "one of life's first needs is for us to be realistic. Don't misunderstand me. We all like you here; you know that. But you've got to be realistic about being a nigger. A lawyer—now that's no realistic goal for a nigger. You've got to think about something you can be. You're good with your hands; you make nice things. You know everybody admires your carpentry show work. Why don't you plan on carpentry?

People really like you as a person. You'd get all kinds of work."

Malcolm could not believe what he was hearing. Mr. Ostrowski had made it a practice to encourage all his students, no matter how farfetched their dreams were. Then Malcolm realized the obvious difference—none of Mr. Ostrowski's other students were black!

Later in life, when Malcolm remembered that afternoon, he would realize the great favor his teacher had done him. At that point in his life he was beginning to realize that the white people he knew didn't look upon him as a friend, or a class president, or a lawyer-to-be or anything like that at all. When they looked at him they saw one thing: his black skin. And people with black skin do not become lawyers, don't get invited to white people's homes, don't talk to white girls. Mr. Ostrowski didn't realize it, but when Malcolm said, "thank you for your answer," he wasn't thanking him for his advice, but rather for the words he had chosen. The division between black and white was clear in Malcolm's eyes. If he was ever to grow and prosper it would have to be as a proud black man, not as a sometimes-accepted member of white society. Boston and Roxbury looked so much more inviting.

The change in Malcolm now became more noticeable every day. Words he had previously ignored, like "nigger" and "coon," became insults to him and he answered them with stinging glares. As a matter of survival in a white-dominated society, Malcolm had been one of the most polite, gentle people around. But he realized that that was the way white people expected him to act, and so he changed. The Malcolm Little that white society liked totally disappeared.

"Tell me what's wrong, Malcolm" became a phrase

he would hear every day, from his teachers and his class-mates, from Mr. and Mrs. Swerlin, and finally from the state welfare representative. But there was no answer Malcolm could give. His own interpretation of what he had to be was in conflict with what the Swerlins expected him to be. There was really only one solution.

Malcolm walked into the Swerlins' living room just in time to hear the state man tell Mrs. Swerlin, "We took your advice under consideration, and as long as he's not happy here we've made arrangements for him to go and stay with another family."

Without another word Malcolm went up to his room and packed his bags. Within a half-hour he was ready to leave. Although he really didn't want to admit it to him-self, he did realize that Mr. and Mrs. Swerlin had been very nice to him. He did his best to hide the tears in his eyes, but Mrs. Swerlin couldn't hide hers. She looked right at him. "Malcolm . . ." she said, but she didn't finish the sentence. There was nothing she could say.

Malcolm stayed with the Lyons family, the only other Negroes in the area, for the two months it took to finish eighth grade. Each weekend he would return to Lansing to visit his brothers and sisters, and he would write Ella at least three times a week. He was terribly lonely for companionship, yet he rejected the attempts at friendship that came from people close at hand. In each letter he would tell Ella how much he loved Boston and how nice it would be to live there. Finally he received the letter he had feared would never come. Somehow Ella had managed to get permission from the state for him to go and live in Massachusetts. For all practical purposes the formal education of Malcolm Little was over. But his real education was just about to begin.

three | *The "New" Malcolm*

BOSTON hadn't changed at all in the few months
Malcolm had spent back in Michigan—it was still as
alive and exciting as ever—but *Malcolm* had changed.
His experiences the previous summer had greatly matured
him. Now he knew just what to expect from Boston and,
more important, how to react to it.

Although by this time Ella had divorced her second
husband, her personality hadn't changed at all. She was
still the independent, proud, commanding figure Malcolm
remembered. The first day of his return she handed him
two keys, one to the door of his own room, the other to
the front door of the house. Instead of the lecture on

responsibility that Malcolm expected to accompany the keys, Ella just said, "Now, Malcolm, don't forget to lock the front door when you leave the house, understand?" Malcolm was on his own.

Together Malcolm and Ella decided it would be best for him to put off getting a job until he felt settled. When the time came, Ella told him, she would make sure that he got a respectable job. Only later did Malcolm realize that to Ella "respectable" meant a job in the Sugar Hill or "upper-class" black area rather than down in the Roxbury ghetto itself. But he was so busy traveling all over the city that he had no time even to think about working.

During his summer visit Malcolm had spent his time seeing the city of Boston itself, but now his interest was in the people that lived there. The first thing that struck him was the way Boston Negroes dressed. In Lansing, clothes had been made with two purposes in mind—to look neat and be strong enough to work in. In Boston clothes were made for show. The first time Malcolm saw a Negro wearing a bright green suit and green patent leather shoes he just stared in disbelief. In all his life he had never seen anything quite so colorful. Although he doubted he would ever own a suit as flashy, within a week he was spending his time staring into store windows and picking his imaginary wardrobe. In his mind Malcolm was decked out just as colorfully as the best dresser in Roxbury. And within a few years Malcolm would turn this dream into reality.

The second thing Malcolm noticed was that most black men in Boston had straight hair, like white people, rather than the curly hair blacks in Lansing had. Although he was trying very hard to play it "cool," Malcolm was totally enthralled by the "sharp cats" who dressed in the brightest colors, dated the best-looking women, didn't seem to work anywhere and spent the better portion of their day standing on street corners.

Ella saw that he was beginning to fall under the influence of the "hip" people and tried to warn him. She much preferred his spending his time with the upper-class Boston blacks on "The Hill" and discouraged him from going down into the ghetto. But in reality there was absolutely nothing she could do about it. Malcolm was not about to take her advice. He was simply overwhelmed by the glitter.

But of all the new discoveries he made, Malcolm was most impressed when he learned how "hip" the young people of the Boston ghetto were. For the first time in his life he saw 10- and 11-year-old kids drinking liquor, smoking cigarettes, gambling with dice, and giving older men money to bet on "the numbers," the most widespread type of gambling in black ghettos. After watching these youngsters for a week Malcolm felt like the oldest teen-ager in the world. He saw Roxbury's pool halls and nightclubs filled with laughing people. Music blared from storefronts and windows twenty-four hours a day. As he walked along the streets Malcolm resigned himself to the fact that he would never belong to the "cool" world that so impressed him.

He was particularly fascinated by the pool halls. He would stand outside the window hypnotized by the sea of green tables with their waves of red, green, blue, orange and yellow balls. Finally, after hours of watching, Malcolm gathered up the courage to go inside. He stood quietly in a corner trying to attract as little attention as possible, making sure he held his stomach in and kept his shoulders squared to look as "cool" as possible.

The pool hall regulars saw right through him. They

had noticed him standing outside and laughed among themselves, and when he stepped inside they totally ignored him. Finally the short, black man that worked there setting up balls walked up to him. "Whattya say, Red," he smiled, referring to Malcolm's bright red hair, "where you from?"

Malcolm tried to look calm, but his excitement caused his voice to break and his answer came out in a high squeak. "Lansing, Michigan."

"Lansing, Michigan!" came the reply. "Well how do you do. That's my hometown too. Now you come on over here with me and tell me about Lansing, Michigan." The rack boy was called Shorty, and he took a liking to Malcolm immediately, never for a second realizing that he was at least ten years older than his new-found friend. The pair sat and talked for over an hour. Finally Shorty told Malcolm he had to go back to work. "Listen Red, is there anything I can do for you?"

"Yes sir, Shorty," came Malcolm's even reply, "I need a job."

Shorty thought for a minute and then shook his head from side to side. "Damn," he finally said, "offhand I can't think of nothing, but let me put the word on the wire. Where can I get ahold of you?" Malcolm gave him Ella's phone number and left. Even before he arrived home Shorty had called to tell him that the shoeshine boy at the Roseland State Ballroom had won a lot of money gambling and was quitting. Malcolm could have the job. All he had to do was report for work the very next night.

Although Ella didn't try to talk him out of taking the job, Malcolm could see that she was not pleased with the type of work he had found. She would have preferred his doing almost anything on the Hill rather than shine the patent leather shoes of the ghetto dwellers in Roseland.

But Malcolm could hardly conceal his excitement. He showed up almost a full hour early the following night, still finding it hard to believe that he was working just a few feet away from the bandstand where Benny Goodman was playing. Benny Goodman! Malcolm thought back to his school dances. They had played the Goodman records over and over, and now here Malcolm was, just a room away from the master himself.

The retiring shoeshine boy gave Malcolm a quick rundown on what he would have to do. Malcolm learned that a few sweeps with a whiskbroom over a suit usually meant a bigger tip, and that by handing out towels he could put more money in his pocket. Selling shoelaces was part of the job too. But, as the shoeshine boy told him, the job included selling some products that had nothing to do with shoes. He was expected to know where his customers could get liquor and marijuana, and he was expected to have contraceptive devices on hand. "With luck and hustling," were the departing shoeshine boy's final words, "you can make ten or twelve bucks a night. The main thing you can't ever forget is that everything in this world is a hustle."

There was one other trade Malcolm learned while working at the shoeshine stand. White women always showed up at black dances, but black ones were forbidden to attend the white-only dances. Malcolm quickly learned that by knowing where white men could find Negro prostitutes he could make quite a bit more than the ten or twelve bucks he had been told about, and he took advantage of the situation. Before long Malcolm had a few "regular customers" who would come up to have their shoes shined just as the dance was ending. As they were leaving, Malcolm would slip a piece of paper with an address on it into their pocket. In exchange these "regulars" would tip him generously for the "shine."

Since he was living with Ella, he had no rent to pay, and at the end of each week he would have more money than he knew what to do with. He had forgotten the lessons of right and wrong preached by his father long ago. He had started smoking marijuana cigarettes, which were called "reefers," drinking liquor, and gambling away a good portion of whatever money was left. The few dollars he did manage to save went into his secret hiding place. There was only one thing Malcolm really wanted—his own "zoot suit," with wide, wide pants, an oversized sports jacket and a long key chain hanging down from the vest. And he intended to buy this dream suit with his savings.

"Savings!" Shorty practically screamed when Malcolm told him of his plan, "Are you kidding? Daddy-O, ain't you never heard of credit? Damn, Homeboy, didn't nobody learn you anything?"

Credit. The buy-now-pay-later plan Earl Little had warned his family against. When Shorty led him downtown to a men's store Malcolm easily forgot his father's warning, and the two of them arranged credit and picked out Malcolm's first zoot suit. He was as proud as a peacock, and that was just about what he looked like in his bright blue pants, his flaring sports jacket, and his blue hat with a feather in it, with the entire outfit topped off by a long gold chain.

"Wow," Malcolm said, "that credit is sure something. It sure is."

The only difference now between Malcolm and the sharpies on the corner was his curly hair. He asked Shorty about it. "It's like this," Shorty told him, "you just got to get it conked, man, that's all."

"Getting conked," Malcolm found, meant using a home-made mixture to straighten out curly hair, which was something done by all "cool" Boston Negroes. When Shorty offered to give him his first conk Malcolm jumped at the chance.

The list of ingredients Malcolm had to buy to make the "congolene" that was used in the conking process sounded like something devised by a mad scientist: 1 can of lye, 2 eggs, 2 potatoes, 1 jar of vaseline, 1 bar of soap, 2 combs, a rubber hose with a metal head, a rubber apron and a pair of rubber gloves.

And what Shorty did with these materials was even worse. After first peeling and slicing the potatoes thin, he put them in a jar and added the acidlike lye. Then he threw in the two eggs. The material started to sizzle, and the jar became so hot that Shorty had to put on the rubber gloves before he could touch it. "You're not going to put that on my head?" asked the unbelieving Malcolm.

"What are you," Shorty answered, "some kind of baby? Like I told you before, when I put this stuff on your head it's really gonna burn—but remember, the longer you can stand the pain the straighter your hair will be. Now just sit down right here."

Malcolm did, and Shorty reached around and tied the rubber vest around his neck. Then he covered Malcolm's head, ears and neck with vaseline. Finally he grabbed a gob of the congolene and put it on Malcolm's head. The whole world caught fire. Malcolm could not believe the pain the still-sizzling material caused. When Shorty took the comb and ran it through Malcolm's hair Malcolm started screaming. He thought his entire skull was coming off. "Get it off! Get it off!"

Shorty was laughing as he washed and then re-washed and again rewashed Malcolm's scalp. Eventually he managed to get all the congolene out and began rubbing on some more vaseline.

"Homeboy," he laughed as he finished up the job, "you sure can yell. There, it's finished."

Malcolm got up very slowly and looked in the mirror. He couldn't believe it—his own conk His very own conk! No white man in the world had hair any straighter than Malcolm's. He felt fifty feet tall. All the adjectives of the street, hip, sharp, smooth, cool, every word fit Malcolm perfectly. He just stared at himself in the mirror. "Damn," he said to Shorty, "that's the best-looking conk I've ever seen. But I sure am glad the second one doesn't hurt as much as the first." Then he laughed.

But when Malcolm looked back on this episode years later he would do so with great shame. He remembered how proud he was of his conk. How for days he had walked around with his head thrust outward as if to say, "Look at me. Look at my conk." What he was really saying, Malcolm was eventually to realize, was, "Look how white I can make myself." What it really proved was that he was ashamed of his race.

But with his conk Malcolm had become part of the street-corner society of Roxbury. He looked like the young hipsters and he spoke like them. And each night Shorty would take him to another great party where he would smoke reefers and drink. He was smoking marijuana regularly now; but most important, as far as he was concerned, he had become one of the best dancers in Roxbury. In the society he was part of, that was not an achievement to be taken lightly. Wherever he went he would lindy-hop his feet off, often to the cheers of a watching crowd. By the end of a typical night the sweat would be pouring down his back. Those moments in the center of the floor, surrounded by an audience, were all he lived for. Coming off the dance floor Malcolm was convinced he was unbeatable in anything he tried.

In one of these carefree moods he quit his job. With money in his pocket and all his sharp friends, Malcolm knew he could find work whenever he wanted it. He decided that he didn't want to be "Red the shoeshine boy," so he walked into the manager's office, threw his rag on the desk and announced that he was quitting. When he went to Roseland now it would be as a fancy-dressed customer, he thought, knocking everyone over with his dazzling dance steps.

Slowly his money disappeared. Needing coin to keep himself in liquor and marijuana, he took a job as a soda-jerk, but he worked as much to pass the hours until the neon lights went on and the bands started playing as he did to raise money.

For Malcolm, dancing had become the most important thing in the world. In reality, though, what mattered was not the dancing but that being a good dancer would give him status. Wherever Malcolm went he would see what values were important to the society he wanted to be part of, then make those values his own. In school, status had been good marks and Malcolm had risen to the top of his class. Here in Boston it was dancing, and few people could put on as good a show.

It was at one of these big dances that Malcolm gazed across the room and saw a pretty white woman looking back at him. Although he had often fixed up black and white men and women, he himself had never gone out with a white woman. It was obvious by the way she looked at him that she was interested. Malcolm returned her stare. The biggest status symbol in the community, even more important than dancing, was dating a white woman. To Malcolm this white girl, whom he called Sophia, was to be nothing more than another trophy in his quest to be the whitest black man in Roxbury.

Just as he thought, Sophia was indeed attracted to Malcolm. What's more, she had a big car and plenty of money. Malcolm made good use of both of them. He often wondered if she would have given him as much as she did if she had known he was only 16 years old.

"Owning" Sophia gave Malcolm a status in Roxbury he had never had before. Having a pretty white woman with him raised Malcolm from the ranks of street corner hustlers to the "very-important-people" category in Roxbury. Soon everyone knew his nickname, and wherever he went someone would be sure to shout out, "Hey Red, what's happening, baby?" He began to get first word of any ghetto news. People he had admired from the day he got off the bus started coming to him to make connections in women and drugs. He was riding high and fancy. He could not conceive of anything important enough to ruin his good life.

He was wrong. On the morning of December 7, 1941, while Malcolm was busy working in Roxbury as a busboy, Japanese planes bombed Pearl Harbor and the easy life was gone. America prepared for war.

Malcolm didn't worry about being drafted because he was still two years underage. Chances were he would have refused to go anyway. Years later, when America was drafting men to fight in Vietnam, Malcolm told his followers, "The black man has died under the flag. His women have been raped under it. I'll do my fighting right here at home, where the enemy looks me in my eye every day of my life. I'm not talking against the flag, I'm talking about it."

Being underage and looking older was a distinct advantage as 1942 began. With tens of thousands of men marching off to war, jobs in every industry went begging. Malcolm could have his choice of almost anything he wanted to do. After careful consideration, it was the lure of the railroad and its promise of travel to the big cities up and down the East Coast that attracted him. Because the railroads so desperately needed porters, a job traditionally held by Negroes, railroad personnel people accepted Malcolm's word that he was over 21.

The railroads. The *20th Century Limited.* The *California Zephyr.* The *Broadway Limited.* The *Wabash Cannonball.* The *Superchief.* Modern America depends on its mammoth airliners for fast, efficient transportation, but in the early forties it was the railroads that captured the most adventurous imaginations. To Malcolm a railroad job was a way of expanding his boundaries, of seeing new places and people, of learning new things. To a teen-ager a railroad job was a dream come true, and Malcolm was no different. He snapped the job up as quickly as he could.

For his first few weeks on the big passenger coaches Malcolm was assigned to work on the *Colonial,* which ran between Boston and Washington, D.C. Although he spent most of his off hours sightseeing in Washington, it didn't overwhelm him the way Boston had. In fact, he began to believe that he had learned too much in the last year ever again to be as overcome with excitement as he was on his first trip to Boston. The moment he set foot in New York City he knew he had been wrong.

When the railroad line's personnel director asked Malcolm if he would like temporarily to replace a porter on the *Yankee Clipper,* which ran from Boston to New York, Malcolm agreed, but only if the man would promise he could have his old job back when he wanted it. He had only to spend a few days in New York City to realize how unnecessary this request was.

As Boston had been to Lansing for Malcolm, so New York was to Boston. It was bigger and more crowded and more colorful. There were more lights and bigger buildings and louder music. The girls were prettier, the men more sophisticated, the zoot suits more plentiful. The multicolored, crazy-shaped neon lights turned night into day. The hundreds of nightclubs made night the time to be out on the streets and day the time to sleep. The moment Malcolm saw Harlem, he knew he was home. Everything that had happened in his life had merely been a preparation for his first day in Harlem.

On the advice of friends who had been to New York, Malcolm's first stop was the nationally famous night spot Small's Paradise. Without consciously realizing it, Malcolm was now laying the groundwork for the next few years of his life. When he arrived at Small's, in the early evening, the Paradise crowd consisted mainly of those who had just completed their day's work, the men who ran the Harlem "numbers" game—and those who were about to begin working, the "pimps" who would spend the rest of the evening finding customers for the prostitutes they "owned." These were the hustlers of Harlem. Malcolm watched them in awe and envy. He had seen nothing like the Small's crowd anywhere in Boston. But within two years he would be part of this very crowd.

From Small's Malcolm went over a few blocks to the Savoy Ballroom, a dance palace that truly lived up to the name. Once a week the poverty-stricken blacks of New York would put on their best clothes and head for the Savoy to "stomp" their troubles away. There was no place like it anywhere. The Savoy Ballroom was the home of some of the greatest names in American musical history: Lionel Hampton, Dizzy Gillespie, Louie Armstrong and Billie Holiday. To Malcolm, Harlem was the biggest, brightest, longest-lasting carnival he had ever seen—and he promised himself that someday he would be ringmaster.

In order to keep his job on the "Clipper," Malcolm became the best porter around. He would walk up and down the aisle performing his tasks efficiently and—most important as far as the railroad was concerned—selling a great number of sandwiches. Eventually the job became his to keep, and he managed to combine what he considered the two perfect worlds, commuting between his first love, Boston, where Sophia waited at the end of each trip, and his new flame, New York.

But all was not well with the railroad. Malcolm was slowly making a bad reputation for himself among trainmen. He tried to make up for being younger than most of the men by being tougher. Every other sound out of his mouth was a curseword, and even those who had been with the railroad thirty or forty years had to think hard to remember anyone quite so fresh as "Red."

Finally, as was bound to happen, Malcolm said the wrong thing at the wrong time. He made a nasty remark to a small but very tough-looking white soldier. The soldier looked up at him and said, so that everyone in the car could hear, "I'm going to fight you, nigger. I'm going to teach you your place."

Malcolm realized that fighting with a passenger would cost him his job. He didn't know exactly what to do, so he tried to put off the battle. "Okay," he said, "I'll fight you, soldier, but not with all those clothes you've got on." The soldier took his coat off.

"Okay Blackie," he challenged, "now let's go."

"But you've still got too many clothes on, "Malcolm pleaded, "all those jackets and stuff." The soldier untied his tie and took his shirt off.

"Now!" he demanded.

"I just can't fight you with all those duds you got on," Malcolm protested, and as soon as the soldier loosened his belt everyone in the car understood what Malcolm was trying to do. They started laughing, quietly at first, then loudly. Finally some of the soldier's friends stopped his undressing act and made him sit down. Malcolm had learned another important lesson. Without raising a finger he had done more damage to that soldier than he could possibly have done with a club. He had made the soldier look like a fool.

But as he walked down the aisle a question gnawed at his mind: "If it had come to actual fighting," he wondered, "would I have fought him?" The chances were he would have. As he was to say years later, "We will never start trouble, but no longer will we turn the other cheek."

Life for Malcolm was one continual whirl. One day he would be parading Sophia in her bright new convertible through Roxbury; the next, he'd be jiving at Small's in Harlem. In his dress he had become as hip as the wildest characters he had ever seen—with a bright green zoot suit, orange shoes, and his hair conked so straight that it looked like a wig. In his daily habits he had almost passed the point of respectability. He smoked marijuana constantly and was continually high. His language was a strange combination of "jive talk" and oaths. Money was something to be spent as quickly as possible. Malcolm never took the time to think about what tomorrow would bring—he was too busy living for today. Even when he was fired by the railroad for his language and attitude, he wouldn't consider changing. He knew jobs were plentiful.

After leaving the railroad he decided to take a trip back to Michigan to visit his family. He walked in un-announced, and his own brothers and sisters almost didn't recognize him. They were so flabbergasted that they didn't know what to say. This was indeed a new Malcolm, and no one was sure the change was for the good.

Once back in New York, getting another job was as simple as stopping at the nearest railroad hiring office. This time Malcolm's train went from New York City to Miami, but the result was no different. His bad attitude caused him to be fired within a few weeks. Malcolm began looking around for somewhere else to work.

The opportunity presented itself almost immediately, and Malcolm was hired as a waiter at Small's Paradise. This was even better than a train job as far as Malcolm was concerned. The only thing that could possibly be better than being a waiter at Small's was being a big shot there. Malcolm assured himself that this would only be a matter of time.

He decided to take advantage of his job and study the people who hung around the place all day. He knew he could learn from them. So he dedicated himself to being the best waiter at Small's, and just as he had done wherever he went, he quickly established a name for himself.

Up until this point everything had gone well for Malcolm. Everything he had hoped for had come true. And, for at least a little while longer things would continue to go in what he thought was the "right" direction. Then the pendulum would begin swinging back the other way—and he would pay for all his good times.

four | *Downfall*

SMALL'S nightclub was indeed a paradise for Malcolm. Every important person in Harlem, the "Who's Who of Black America," made it a point to stop in at Small's as often as possible. Malcolm tried to figure out when the most important people would be there and would always arrange his work schedule so that he could be on hand to serve them. And serve them he did! Like a flash he was back and forth from the kitchen or bar with his customers' orders; as soon as someone took a cigarette out of his pocket Malcolm would pop up to light it; and if anyone ever had even a slight problem he would be there with the solution.

In this way he began attracting the attention of the Harlem hustlers he so admired. In time, he began learning the tricks of their trades. From the dope peddlers he learned how to pick out a policeman in a crowd; from the men who made their living selling women he learned how to recruit prostitutes to work for him; he learned the important things to know about running a gambling operation; and finally, from those who had graduated from street hustling into big-time crime, he learned how to plan and conduct house burglaries. Malcolm listened carefully and remembered everything he was told. If he was ever to reign at one of Small's tables he would have to learn these lessons well.

But for the present at least, Malcolm was very happy. He enjoyed his job so much that he was almost willing to work for nothing. And, when he considered it, with all the money he was spending on marijuana and the "numbers," nothing was what he had left at the end of the week. "The numbers," with its promise of instant wealth, was his new love.

"Numbers" is a type of gambling extremely popular in poverty areas because, for a bet as small as a penny, there is the hope of a "big hit." In most of America's ghettos millions and millions of dollars are bet every day.

It works this way. A person bets whatever amount he wants on a specific three-digit number. The "winning number" for the day is based on something no single person can control, such as the last three numbers of the total number of stocks sold on the New York Stock Exchange in a single day. If the number you select is 317 and next day the newspaper says 2,769,317 stocks were sold the day before, you've "hit" the number and are a winner. The amount you win depends on how much you originally bet multiplied by 600. On a 50-cent bet the pay off would be $300; on a dollar bet, $600.

On the rare occasions when someone did win, the news spread rapidly around the neighborhood, and you could be sure everyone would bet a little extra money the next day. Fortunes had been made in a single day, and everyone who bet was convinced that he would be the next person to "hit it." Although no one really knows how much money is bet nationally on the numbers each day, there is no doubt that "numbers" is a multimillion-dollar business.

What number to pick? The last three numbers of a license plate, something that appears to you in a dream, a page in a book, the date of your birth—it really makes no difference. The numbers is a game with thousands of losers and only one guaranteed winner every day: the man who runs the operation! But the fact that the odds are overwhelmingly against the bettor hasn't stopped many from risking their money.

But directing players to a numbers "runner," who would take the bets, was only one of the things Malcolm did as a waiter at Small's. Once he discovered which of the regular customers at Small's were undercover policemen, he had little fear of occasionally directing another customer to one of the prostitutes who lived in his building. By this time Malcolm, who was known throughout Harlem as "Detroit Red," knew just what he wanted: the fast life and plenty of money. He no longer worried about what was right and what was wrong; he had left his morals back in Boston. Now, as far as Malcolm was concerned, it was just a matter of finding the right "hustle."

He was forced to find it sooner than he wanted.

While working at the Paradise one afternoon he leaned across a table and asked a black serviceman if he was looking for a prostitute. "If you are," Malcolm said to him, "I think I can help you out." To Malcolm's amazement the soldier turned out to be an undercover agent for Army Intelligence. Within an hour the New York City police showed up and had taken Malcolm into custody. Because he was "clean"—meaning that he had never been arrested before—the police decided to throw a scare into him and then release him. So they brought him into a small room and began screaming at him, calling him names and threatening all sorts of punishment. Finally they just looked up, laughed and said, "Beat it, kid. And don't let us see you here again." Malcolm wasted no time getting out of there.

The owner of Small's was not so forgiving. He had a business to run and couldn't risk further incidents. Malcolm was fired and forbidden ever to enter Small's Paradise again. To Malcolm that was almost worse than a prison sentence.

But hustlers of the type he wanted to be are a strange breed. Although each claims to be totally independent, there is a strong bond of camaraderie among men who live beyond the limits of the law. So, when Malcolm was fired, some of his former customers—people who saw him as a successful hustler-to-be—offered to help him. Sammy the Pimp, who was eventually to become his best friend, suggested to Malcolm that he might make a lot of money selling marijuana. Like just about everything else he tried, Malcolm was immediately successful as a "grass" salesman. Within a month he was making sixty dollars a day for only a few hours' work. Best of all, there was actually very little risk involved.

Malcolm was careful never to sell his product to anyone he didn't know beforehand or who was not specifically recommended by one of his other customers.

More quickly than he thought possible, Malcolm changed from someone who watched the Harlem hustlers in awe to a member-of-the-group. He couldn't spend his money fast enough. He went to Boston to see Sophia and Ella. He bought new suits, this time a little more conservative to fit his new, mature image. And he also figured that there was no need to attract extra attention. He sent money to his brothers Reginald and Philbert and to the rest of the Little family still back in Michigan. And, most important of all, he bought more marijuana, so he could stay in business.

His reputation spread in Harlem. He became "Detroit Red, the man with the good stuff," and had so many customers that they almost had to stand in line outside his door. Of course, in addition to customers, the police began to notice him too. In many cases individual policemen had made "deals" with Harlem pushers: they would leave them alone in return for a small percentage of the profits. Malcolm, independent as always, refused to make any such deals. And so he was now in competition both with other sellers and the policemen they dealt with—so both groups wanted him out of the way. The police began to trail him constantly, and he had to spend more and more time evading their watchful eyes. He began to sell less and less. His regular customers, hearing through the Harlem grapevine that Malcolm was being watched, began shying away from him. Business was getting bad.

One afternoon Malcolm returned to his apartment and discovered that someone had been there while he was gone and had searched through all his belongings. Since none of his valuables were missing he figured it must have been the police, and so he began moving from apartment to apartment every few months. He also began carrying a small gun. Although he told himself he was only carrying it for protection, he realized that he would not hesitate to use it if the police got too close.

But the biggest problem was the state of his business: it just continued to get worse and worse. Every time he looked over his shoulder he spotted a policeman or plainclothesman following him. His money began to run short, and he was now trapped in a cycle. He couldn't buy marijuana because he didn't have money, and he couldn't make money because he had no marijuana to sell. Finally he ran out of money for his trips to Boston and for his folks in Michigan. There were no more new suits. Now it was a matter of survival. Money for food. Money for rent.

He started to borrow, a little here, a little there, just enough to keep him going. The other hustlers, the men who had helped him when he first started, wanted nothing to do with him. The word was out: Malcolm was "hot." The police wanted to catch him doing almost anything illegal, and the other hustlers stayed far away from him.

In desperation Malcolm turned to Sammy for advice. Sammy thought for a moment, then said, "You know Red, as far as I can see, the best thing for you would be to get out of Harlem."

"Sure," Malcolm answered bitterly, "but what am I going to do, walk to Boston?" With that he reached in his pocket, pulled out his wallet, turned it upside down, and shook it. The only things that fell out were a few cards. Malcolm was dead broke. He couldn't find a single penny. Sammy bent down to the sidewalk and picked up one of the cards.

"How 'bout this one?" he asked, holding out Malcolm's old railroad identification card. The new hustle Sammy suggested was really a combination of two of Malcolm's old ones. Using his old ID card, he would travel up and down the East Coast, selling marijuana to members of the big bands that constantly traveled and were rarely in any town long enough to make a contact. Since he had gotten to know a great many of the musicians personally while working at Small's and Boston's Roseland, he expected to do a steady business. He was right. Within a month he was out of debt and things were looking bright again.

"Sammy," he said to his friend, as the two sat in his Harlem apartment smoking marijuana one afternoon, "this has gotta be the best hustle anyone ever had. Imagine, traveling all around the country listening to great music every place you stop and making money at it. There ain't nothin' can go wrong now."

As was happening more and more now, Malcolm was dead wrong. One morning he came home from a trip to find a single letter waiting for him. He took one look at the envelope and knew it was trouble. "Greetings from the President of the United States . . ." it began. Malcolm had been ordered to report for his Army physical.

What to do? Malcolm had long ago decided he would not serve in the Army, but how was he going to get out of it? He called Sammy, but Sammy told him that this was one rap he didn't know how to beat. He called some of his other friends. Again, no one knew how to beat Uncle Sam. "When he puts the finger on you," Malcolm was told, "you is elected!" But he refused to give up and, sure enough, he came up with a plan.

The first thing he did was take his old zoot suit out of the closet and start wearing it again. Then he began going places he knew were frequented by Army under-cover agents. In a loud voice he said one crazy thing after another, acting like a man totally under the influence of drugs. He hoped word of his actions would get back to the Army doctors who were to examine him. It did, and when he went for his physical he was pulled out of line and taken to the office of the Army psychiatrist. After a short wait he was ushered into the doctor's office.

The office was small but neat. Malcolm walked across the room and took a chair directly facing the white-coated Army "head-shrinker," the slang term everyone used for a psychiatrist. He folded his hands on his lap and looked directly at the doctor. The doctor folded his hands and stared back at Malcolm. Neither said a word. Finally the doctor swung his chair around so his back was to Malcolm, and picked up a folder. "Malcolm," he said, swinging his chair back around, "I just want to ask you a few questions. Before you answer this, remember, I'm here to be your friend. Now, the first question is, do you want to be in the Army?"

Malcolm paused for effect; long ago he had decided exactly what he was going to say. Leaning forward, he looked carefully around the room. He got up from his chair, walked to the door, tested it to see that it was closed, then got down on his hands and knees and peered under it. "It's okay," he said. Then, still on his hands and knees, he went across the room to the only closet in

the room. Again, he peered under the door. "It's okay,"
he said to the doctor.

Finally he got up and walked back to his chair.
"You can never be too careful, you know." Then he
leaned forward and in a voice barely louder than a
whisper said to the "shrink," "Now, I wouldn't tell you
this normally, but since you say we're friends I guess
it's okay. You bet I wanna be in the Army. Daddy-O,
now you and me, we're from up North here, so you
won't tell anybody . . . I want to get in that old Army
and I want to get down South. Organize them nigger
soldiers—you dig? Steal us some guns and kill up them
southern crackers!"

The Doctor gaped at him, and needless to say,
within an hour Malcolm had been classified as an Army
reject. But he himself was thinking, as he left the exam-
ination center a free man, that in reality it was Malcolm
who had rejected the Army!

Now that the Army had been successfully avoided,
Malcolm returned to his "traveling salesman" job. But
one evening he was unwise enough to get involved in
a high stakes card game on one of the railroad lines.
The game ended in a fight and, to protect himself and
his winnings, Malcolm made the mistake of pulling his
gun.

He kept the money but lost the use of his railroad
ID card. The word spread among trainmen, "Keep the
red-headed Negro off the trains." Again Malcolm was
left without a hustle. The only thing he knew how to do
well was sell drugs, and Harlem had become too dangerous for him to sell there.

"Looking back," he once said, "I had become the
true hustler—uneducated, unskilled at anything honor-

able, and I considered myself nervy and cunning enough to live by my wits, exploiting any prey that presented itself. I would risk just about anything now."

The step into robbery was an easy one for him to take, and he talked Sammy into helping him pull some small jobs. Malcolm made it a point to get very high on drugs before he went "to work." This solved two problems: he would not be at all nervous when breaking into the place being robbed, and the drugs covered any pangs of conscience he might have had. The gun had now become part of his daily uniform.

The partnership with Sammy lasted about six months. It came to an abrupt halt when a watchman discovered the pair in the midst of a job. "Stop or I'll shoot," he warned. Malcolm and Sammy took off and the watchman did shoot, winging Sammy in the arm. Unharmed, Malcolm dropped Sammy off at his own apartment and then went home.

Later that night he returned to Sammy's place to see how he was. The woman Sammy was living with at the time blamed his injured arm on Malcolm and started hitting him. When Malcolm hit her back Sammy became enraged and a fight broke out between the two partners. For all practical purposes, both the partnership and the friendship had come to an end.

Deciding that burglary was too dangerous, Malcolm began to look around for another hustle. There was only one thing he hadn't tried, the numbers. Through some of his old connections he got a job as a "runner" and went into the streets to collect the nickels, dimes and dollars. Now he had been involved in just about all the street hustles—prostitution, dope-peddling, robbery and the numbers. There was really only one way things could turn out and he began to realize that it was only a matter of time before he came face to face with the law.

But he hadn't quite reached bottom yet. Whenever things started to go bad, Malcolm would take the easiest way out, an escape into his drug-produced dreamland. He was beginning to rely more and more on marijuana, smoking it from the time he woke up until he went to sleep. He also began experimenting with drugs like opium and cocaine on a regular basis.

His luck, which had been good for such a long time, finally turned sour. A Negro bar was held up by a man fitting Malcolm's general description. Instead of calling the police, the owner of the bar hired a gang of black toughs to find the holdup man. Malcolm, innocent this time, just barely made it out of Harlem without being caught. He returned in about a week, just in time to hear that an uptown dice game had been held up, again by a man fitting his general description. And once again a group of strong-arm men went looking for the holdup man.

The only bright spot in the world, Malcolm thought, came when he hit the "number" for $300. "Now," Malcolm told a friend of his, "my luck is starting to change again." How wrong he was.

Under the influence of drugs Malcolm had mixed up his numbers. The number he claimed to hold was not actually the one he had bet on. West Indian Archie, the gambler who had paid off the $300, wanted his money back, and he wanted it quickly. Malcolm probably would have returned the money, but he had spent every penny of it on a huge celebration. Now it was impossible to raise that much money.

"Twenty-four hours," Archie told him, "or else

we'll have to talk in another language!" From the look on his face and the gun tucked into his belt, Malcolm knew exactly what he meant.

There were only two choices open to Malcolm: he could either leave Harlem or stay and fight. Leaving now, he knew, would be an admission of guilt and he would never again be welcome, yet to stay meant he would have to fight it out with a popular sixty-year-old Harlem figure.

As he had done so many times before when the problem had become too hard to solve, Malcolm turned to drugs. Only this time it was not a matter of just getting high; this time he set out to destroy himself. He started with marijuana, then switched to opium, smoking that with an actor friend until he could no longer maintain his balance. Then he smoked some more marijuana. Then he went over to Sammy's house and the two, now reunited, took some cocaine. By now Malcolm had lost all contact with reality. His mind had long ceased functioning normally, and it seemed only a matter of hours until the unavoidable crash with reality. This time there didn't seem the slightest possibility he would escape his fate.

But, somehow, he still had a little luck left. While staggering along St. Nicholas Avenue Malcolm heard a horn honk. There, right in the middle of New York City, was Shorty. When word had reached Boston that Malcolm was in serious trouble, Shorty had borrowed a car and driven down to help out.

"What's happening, Red?"

"Oh, nothin' much, Daddy-O," Malcolm answered.

"Wanna come back to the Hill with me?"

Malcolm laughed, "Why not?" then climbed into the

back seat of the car and collapsed. Shorty made a U-turn around a traffic island and headed back to Boston. It was the last time Malcolm would see his beloved Harlem for many years.

He had now completed the cycle from high popularity to the gutter. "Back then," he once explained, "I believed that a man should do anything he was slick enough, or bad or bold enough, to do. A woman was nothing but something to own. Every word I spoke was either hip or a curseword. I would bet my vocabulary wasn't two hundred words."

When he woke in Shorty's apartment, Malcolm realized one important thing: he had become a dope addict. He found he couldn't live without being high on one drug or another. "I viewed narcotics as most people viewed food"—and for him indeed they had become just as necessary as food. But drugs are expensive to start with, and the people who sell them tend to price them according to how badly an individual needs them. If you can live without drugs they are relatively inexpensive, but when you become addicted and need them badly the price goes sky high. And this was the story as far as Malcolm was concerned. When dealers saw how badly off he was, they priced their drugs accordingly. Money had again become a major problem. He needed a lot of it, and fast. Unfortunately, the quickest way he knew was also the most dangerous, house burglary.

Malcolm and Shorty decided to organize a little band of robbers. They recruited a friend of Shorty's named Rudy. Malcolm remembered the lessons learned in Small's. In order to make a team he needed "finders," people who could look over the layout of the planned robbery without attracting attention. For this job Malcolm recruited his old girlfriend, Sophia, and her younger sister, who by now was dating Shorty. The girls' role was to scout white neighborhoods and find "easy" jobs. Malcolm knew these white girls would attract very little suspicion in white neighborhoods, and that is where he sent them. After the girls had found a house, drawn a picture of the layout and uncovered some basic information, such as the hours when the owners would not be there, Malcolm and Shorty would pull the job. Rudy would drive the getaway car.

The night before the gang was scheduled to pull its first job, the five of them met in a room in Cambridge, Massachusetts, that the girls had rented. Malcolm sat on a bed across from the four others, playing lazily with his gun. Finally he took the gun and shook out all five bullets. With the other four watching, he held up a single bullet and put it back in the gun, twirled the muzzle and lifted the gun to his head. As the other four watched in terror, Malcolm pulled the trigger.

Click! Nothing happened. Again he pulled the trigger. *Click!* Now only three chambers were left, and one of them had a bullet in it. The odds were getting smaller.

"Stop it!" Shorty screamed and ran across the room to grab the gun. Malcolm stared him down.

"I did that to show you that I'm not afraid to die. Remember this: never cross a man who is not afraid to die." With his simple dramatics Malcolm had eliminated all doubt as to who was the leader of the gang. And dramatics is the right word, for the whole thing had been an act. What the rest of them didn't know was that Malcolm had given them a demonstration of something he had learned long ago on a dirt road in Lansing, Michigan. Never gamble unless it's a sure thing. And, in this case, he knew he was betting on a sure thing. Without any of the others, realizing it, he had pocketed the extra bullet. He had been in absolutely no danger when he pulled the trigger of the gun.

The next night the first job went off even more smoothly than any of them had dared hope. The second robbery was a repeat performance of the first. So was the third, the fourth, and the fifth . . . The group pulled the job, sold the stolen loot, then lay low until the money was spent. It was an old rule: never go after more than you need. But Malcolm's tastes were improving about as quickly as his drug habit was getting worse, and so he needed more and more money. The jobs came a lot more frequently than they had at the beginning, and a lot less planning went into each. The gang had fallen into a routine. They would go into the suburbs, pull a job, contact their "fence" (the man who bought the goods from them at a low price and resold them at a profit), and quickly spend the money they received. For Malcolm, spending was the easiest part of it. Life had indeed become very simple for him. He had no real job to worry about, no family to support, no responsibilities. He had indeed become a full-fledged "upper-class" citizen of the hustler's world.

It had to end. Malcolm's drugs eventually caused him to become careless. He had kept a watch, taken from a Boston mansion, for himself. The watch was broken, though, and Malcolm brought it into a jewelry repair shop. That was his downfall. Since the watch was somewhat rare, and the owner knew it was broken, the police knew exactly what to look for. Boston police had alerted all jewelry shops in the area to be on the lookout for that watch. Minutes after Malcolm had brought it in, the shop owner was on the phone with the police, and they were waiting for Malcolm when he walked in to pick it up. His luck had finally run out.

I N an American courtroom the judge sits on a chair raised high above the rest of the people in the room. The reason is simple. He is acting not as an individual but as the representative of truth and justice. In order to see him, an individual must raise his head, a sign of respect. The way Malcolm felt, however, the judge could have been squatting on the floor and Malcolm still would have had to look up to see him.

Malcolm had finally come out of his drug-produced trance and was beginning to realize that he was in a very serious situation. This time Ella would not be able to come to his aid; this time there was no escape. The trial had gone swiftly and Malcolm had been found guilty.

The fact that the jury knew he was living with a white girl, Malcolm thought, would not make things any easier for him. The judge looked down at him and asked, "Do you have anything to say before I pronounce sentence?"

For the first time in as long as he could remember, Malcolm had absolutely nothing to say.

"Then," said the judge, "by the powers vested in me by the State of Massachusetts I hereby sentence you to not less than five nor more than ten years in a suitable state prison." Ten years! An entire decade to remember how "cool" he had been. Ten long years. His lawyer was deeply surprised; even he had not expected such a severe sentence. He didn't understand why the judge had been so harsh.

Malcolm did. In his own mind he knew he had been convicted of two crimes, not one: robbery and living with Sophia. He also knew there was only one escape. He had to get some dope and end this nightmare. But he couldn't, at least not right away.

Malcolm was sent to Charleston State Prison to begin his sentence. Charleston State had been built in 1805 and should have been torn down many years before Malcolm arrived there. The cells were so small that he would lie with his head against one wall and his feet firmly against the other. The only bathroom facilities available to prisoners were the covered pails, one in the corner of each cell. But after a few weeks in prison Malcolm began to "case the place" and think about how he could take charge. He tried to make small inroads and gain some leadership. For the first time he was not at all successful.

Prison society is very strict. It is indeed a place where the strong survive and become leaders. Malcolm was a newcomer to prison life, and those who had spent many years behind bars were not about to let any "new boy" gain control. Since they wouldn't let him "join" their society, Malcolm decided to start his own. It would consist of only the meanest and toughest men at Charleston. He would set an example and let those who liked what they saw come to him.

So he became meaner than the meanest prisoner, tougher than the toughest. When the guards came with his food he would curse and throw the tray at them. His language, never good, got progressively worse. He lashed out at everything and anything. But there was still a piece missing. In every other situation Malcolm had been involved with, there was always some person, a single individual, on whom Malcolm could place all the blame. Now there was none, and though he tried to create some enemy he could fight, there was really no one but himself to blame. So he turned on the one thing that couldn't fight back, religion.

He began ranting and raving at "that God" who had put him in jail. Every other word out of his mouth was a curse aimed at belittling God and all organized religions. And even though his anger was aimed at religion he took it out on the people he lived with, until it became impossible for him to work with the other prisoners. Because of this attitude the other prisoners gave him a new nickname, Satan. Worse, because of his conduct he was isolated in solitary confinement.

But all the time Malcolm was shooting off his mouth and causing trouble he was watching and learning too. He was trying to figure out the easiest angle, the quickest way to gain control. Among other things he noticed, and would remember, is that certain things were the same behind bars as they were on the outside. On the whole, he found, white prisoners were treated much better than black ones by white guards. Even in prison, he thought, this is a white society. When there was a bad job to be done, the guards would almost always pick a black prisoner. On the other hand, white inmates always got the good jobs. The black prisoners were also expected to listen to orders given them by white prisoners. There was only a single exception, an elderly black prisoner known as Bimbi.

After the day's work had been completed, a large number of inmates, both black and white, as well as some of the guards, would cluster around in a large circle, and Bimbi would hold court. He would talk about almost anything: history, religion, philosophy, science—anything the other prisoners wanted to know more about. His listeners would sit fascinated until the whistle blew and they had to return to their cells. Malcolm would usually stand on the edge of the group, interested of course, but secretly envious of the attention Bimbi commanded.

Malcolm and Bimbi hardly ever spoke to each other. Malcolm's language consisted of almost all curse-words, and Bimbi never used anything but proper English. In the few conversations the two did have, Malcolm would almost always end up yelling and trying to scare Bimbi into changing his mind. Bimbi never raised his voice. While Malcolm had always believed whoever was stronger was right, Bimbi was winning converts using a calm and reasoned approach. One day, with no warning, Bimbi walked right up to Malcolm and said, "You know boy, you really are a whole lot more intelligent than you let on."

Malcolm was in no mood for advice. "What do you want?" he demanded.

"Want?" Bimbi laughed in Malcolm's face. "Listen,

I don't want anything from you. I just want to tell you that you should take advantage of the time you're going to spend here. It won't go any quicker if you just sit around."

Malcolm mumbled something and walked away, but he couldn't walk away from Bimbi's ideas. He's right, Malcolm finally decided, and it can't hurt to find some new way to pass the hours. He soon discovered the prison library and started taking books out. Then someone told him about the correspondence courses the prison offered. Malcolm figured, What do I have to lose? Nothing. The last time he had been in a classroom was in eighth grade. It seemed like a hundred years ago. Slowly he began reading. The basics he had mastered in school began to come back to him. After almost a year of constant reading and a few writing courses, he began to correspond regularly with his brothers and sisters.

Malcolm did more to imitate Bimbi. He remembered that Bimbi had often fascinated the people around him by discussing the history of words. So on Bimbi's advice he began studying Latin so he would know word derivations himself. As he had thrown himself into hustling on the street, Malcolm slowly began pushing himself into education. Not that he had totally changed, of course; he still ran a number of small hustles, like betting pools for baseball and football. And there was always a guard willing to sell him some marijuana in exchange for part of his winnings.

One of the few bright moments Malcolm had in prison came in 1947. In April of that year a young man named Jack Roosevelt Robinson, playing for the Brooklyn Dodgers, became the first black man to play major league baseball. Jackie Robinson captured the imagination of the American Negro community just as Joe Louis had done, and Malcolm would sit by his radio every day listening for news of how Jackie and the Dodgers had done that day.

Between baseball and his renewed interest in education, Malcolm had little time to be the "toughest and meanest." Because of his improved behavior, as well as the overcrowded condition of the prison at Charleston, Malcolm was transferred to a much better prison in Concord. Soon after his arrival there he received a letter from his brother Philbert. "Dear Brother," the letter began, "I have discovered the natural religion for the black man." Philbert went on to write about something he called "The Nation of Islam." Malcolm, who still considered religion something the white man used to keep the black man "in his place," laughed at his younger brother's letter and tore it up.

A second letter, this time from his brother Reginald, arrived a few days later. "Malcolm," read the letter, "don't eat any more pork and don't smoke any more cigarettes. I'll show you how to get out of prison."

"Get out of prison." Magic words to Malcolm. What could the secret be? How could Malcolm fool the police by not eating pork or smoking cigarettes? What was Reginald's plan? Whatever it was, Malcolm decided, if there was anything he could do to get out of jail one hour sooner, he would do it. That day he gave up cigarettes and pork. As he realized later, he was taking the first steps toward becoming a Muslim—and didn't even know it!

Malcolm realized that whatever plan Reginald had would take time to develop, so he continued to study during most of his free hours. Things changed considerably for the better when Ella managed to get him trans-

ferred again, this time to the Norfolk Prison Colony.
Norfolk was an experimental prison. There were no bars
across the windows and no outside locks on the doors.
The prisoners lived in small groups in clean, modern
buildings. Even better, as far as Malcolm was concerned,
there was total freedom to discuss any topic. Discussion
groups met every evening, and Malcolm was sure to be
found in the middle of one. Teachers would come from
nearby Harvard and Boston University to lead these discussion groups, and, eventually, Malcolm emerged as
one of the leaders. When a prison debating team was
formed, Malcolm was one of the first selected.

Norfolk had a large library donated by a million-
aire. The tens of thousands of books on hand covered
an incredibly large range of topics. Now when people
wanted to talk to Malcolm they knew just where to look,
because he was spending every free moment in the
library.

After what seemed like years, Malcolm received a
letter from Reginald telling him he was coming to visit.
Finally Malcolm would find out what the great scheme
was. He could hardly wait.

The two brothers sat facing each other. Reginald
began by discussing members of the family, news of the
outside—everything but what Malcolm really wanted to
hear. Finally he began talking about Philbert's letter, the
letter Malcolm had torn up. "There is a man who knows
everything," he told Malcolm. "His real name is Allah!"

Malcolm was startled. This was no plan. How was
this going to help him get out of prison?

Reginald went on: "The white man is the devil."

Malcolm thought about this for a moment. "Without any exceptions? Every white man is the devil?" Mal-

colm asked. Reginald nodded. Malcolm didn't really understand. He had known many good white people. And how was any of this going to get him out of prison? He had to have time to think. He asked Reginald to leave and return in a few days.

Alone, Malcolm spent much time in deep thought. When, he asked himself, had a white man ever done anything good for him? In every example he thought about, the white person involved had gained something by helping him. The Swerlins had been paid by the state for keeping him, for example, and he just dismissed Sophia as a not-too-intelligent woman. And who was this fellow Allah? Where did he come from? What did he teach? Where would Malcolm fit in? When Reginald returned, Malcolm asked him all these questions.

Reginald held up his hand. "In time you'll learn it all, Malcolm; in time you'll learn it all."

Reginald began coming more and more often. Letters from other members of the Little family began arriving every day. They had all become members of this "Nation of Islam" Philbert had written about. Slowly, through their letters and Reginald's teaching, Malcolm began to piece together the story of the Muslim nation.

In the summer of 1930 a man by the name of W. D. Fard had appeared in the Negro section of Detroit selling silks and other articles he claimed were imported from Africa. But he became more popular among the Detroit blacks because of his beautiful stories about their African homeland. He also preached against the white race and against the Christian religion. Many people in the ghetto believed what Fard said, and they organized the very first Temple of Islam. Fard later founded the University of Islam, actually a grade school that went all the way to eighth grade, and a group he called the Fruit of Islam. The Fruit of Islam were a group of muscular men assigned to protect Fard and the Temple. But somewhere something went wrong, and in 1934, with no advance word, Fard disappeared, never to be heard from again. He was succeeded by a short black man named Elijah Muhammad.

Muhammad had been born Elijah Poole in Georgia in 1897. After Fard's strange disappearance, Elijah began telling members of the Detroit Temple that Fard had actually been Allah himself, and thus he, Elijah Muhammad, was Allah's messenger. Because he feared that his life was in danger from some of Fard's more militant followers, Muhammad moved to Chicago to organize a second chapter. Allah, he told all who would listen, had come to America as Fard to help put the black man in his chosen place of leadership.

In the beginning, Muhammad taught, the moon was separated from the earth and the original humans, a race of black men and women, were created. They founded the Holy City that is now called Mecca. Each member of this race had two sides to his nature: a black side, which represented the strengths and good habits of man, and a white side, which stood for the bad habits and weaknesses of mortal man. The white race as we know it today was created by a scientist who had been banned from Mecca because of his teachings. To get even, he continually bred light-skinned children until an all-white race was created as his revenge. Whites were then granted 6,070 years. Their time would be up in 1984.

Malcolm was fascinated. He didn't know whether to believe this story or not, but he listened to the suggestions of the members of his family and painstakingly wrote a letter to Elijah Muhammad. Later he found that he was not alone. Black convicts all across America were turning to Elijah Muhammad for guidance. And Muhammad did not fail any of them. He personally answered each letter, telling the prisoner it was not his own fault that he was behind bars, but rather that of the white society that discriminated against the black man. Often, he told the prisoners, the only road open to the black man is the road that leads to crime. And in each letter Muhammad included a five-dollar bill.

Malcolm began to write Muhammad every day. And even though he had started reading and writing daily, his knowledge had never really progressed beyond the eighth-grade level. He became ashamed of his lack of knowledge. As he was first beginning to realize, and would later tell his own followers, the greatest single weapon any man can ever have is real knowledge. The more he knows, the stronger a warrior he is. Once you take a man's knife or club away from him, Malcolm realized, the man becomes totally defenseless, but knowledge is something no one can ever take away. So Malcolm began to search for that total knowledge.

He spent hour after hour, day after day, in the library. After hours, when the lights in the rooms were turned out, he would lie in the corner of his room, reading by the hall lights. But there was a constant problem: so many words he didn't know! On each page there were sure to be at least a couple of sentences with words new to Malcolm. His penmanship was nothing to be proud of, either. Although he now set aside a certain part of each day for writing letters, and sent them to everyone from Reginald to the President of the United States, he was still ashamed of his almost unreadable handwriting. He couldn't even print in a straight line. One day Malcolm came upon a solution to both problems. He discovered how to use the dictionary.

To Malcolm the dictionary was almost a magical book. He knew that if he could learn what was inside its covers he would be able to read and understand any book. So one afternoon he picked up the dictionary and, on a page in his notebook, copied the entire first page word for word. Then he studied it. The next day he copied the second page and then studied that. Slowly he progressed through all the "a's," then through the "b's," the "c's," and so on, right through the entire dictionary! He found it was indeed the magical book he had thought it to be. The dictionary turned out to be an education in itself. It told of history, science, people, places, things —things he had never even dreamed existed. By the time he had reached "z," there were few books he could not pick up and understand. And just as important, his handwriting had become legible.

Although he read books on every subject, he was particularly interested in history. He began to learn things about the black race that he had never imagined. He had never before thought of history except in the terms he was taught in school: white Columbus discovering America, white settlers arriving from Europe and building colonies, the Civil War between whites to abolish slavery. He was amazed to learn that there was a black history predating by far any history he had learned in class. The black man, he read, had built kingdoms in Africa long before anyone ever heard of Columbus. "We once were kings," he thought in amazement.

The books opened his eyes to the horrors of slavery.

He saw drawings of men and women chained and beaten, read stories of families separated and men working from dawn to dusk for no payment and just enough food to survive. With this background the teachings of Muhammad began to make much more sense.

He was not at all surprised to discover that few of the other Negro prisoners knew anything about black history. Like Malcolm, they had given little or no thought to who they were or where they came from. "Think," Malcolm told them, "and then ask yourself who built this prison and put you in here?" There was no need for an answer. Once again Malcolm joined the daily prison debates. But this time, with his new wealth of information, he was the center of attraction. He kept after the other black prisoners to learn something about themselves.

"Would you just leave me alone!" one of them told Malcolm. "What difference does it make?"

Malcolm was amazed. "What difference does it make? You don't even know your real name, where your grandparents came from, or what any of your ancestors were like, and you don't think it makes any difference? You ever hear of Aesop's Fables?" he yelled at him. "I'll bet you have—but I'll bet you didn't know Aesop was a black man. Aesop is only the Greek word for Ethiopian!"

As the weeks passed, Malcolm began to see results. His badgering drove other black prisoners to the library to check out what he told them. He was glad for two reasons: First, it got the men into the library, and second, he was always proved right. He had risen to the top of the Colony's society, no longer the toughest but certainly one of the smartest.

Through the teachings of his family, Malcolm had

almost become a member of the "Nation of Islam," but his formal induction would have to wait until he was out of prison. But he did follow the strict Muslim code and did not drink, smoke, or eat any pork. He no longer cursed, and he wouldn't fight. He could never figure out exactly why he stuck so closely to the codes, at least until he saw the results of a Muslim's breaking them.

His brother Reginald continued to visit him each week, but the tone of his voice had changed. Where he had been lavish in praise of Muhammad and the Muslims for almost five years now, negative ideas began to creep into his conversation. Finally he told Malcolm he thought the entire Muslim nation was a fraud. Malcolm could hardly believe it: Reginald, who had brought him to Islam, was now trying to turn him against it. Why?

Philbert told him. Reginald had been suspended from the Temple of Islam because he was having a love affair with a secretary in violation of a Muslim code against immoral relationships. Malcolm didn't know what to do. He knew he would eventually have to make a decision, would have to choose between his own brother and membership in the Muslims. With nowhere else to go for advice he turned to Elijah Muhammad.

Muhammad's reply was simple and to the point: if Malcolm chose to stick with his brother, all the things he now believed in, his whole new life, would lose their meaning. If he chose the Muslims, he would be able to understand who he was, why he was in prison, what he could make of himself. Malcolm remained undecided until the evidence began to appear before his eyes.

Reginald was indeed a different person. Where he had once been so clean and neat, he now wore dirty tee-shirts and soiled, wrinkled pants. His mental attitude had changed greatly too. He began inventing stories and imagining things. He told Ella he had walked all the way from Detroit to Boston. He began seeing snakes everywhere. He started standing on street corners, preaching to passersby that he had been sent from Allah to save them. Finally, state authorities had to put Reginald in a mental hospital. Malcolm had seen living proof of what happens to one who strays from the Muslim fold. Now, more than ever, he believed in the power of the Muslims to do good for the black man. He vowed to teach as many black people as possible about the great injustices suffered at the hands of the white man. He could hardly wait to get out of prison.

That great moment came almost a year later. Malcolm had gained a reputation at Colony State as someone who could stir up the other black prisoners. In fact, shortly after he had decided Muhammad was right and his brother wrong, Malcolm was transferred back to Charleston. But when he came up for parole the board saw the obvious change in him, and because there was a job waiting for him back in Detroit, they agreed to release him.

With $10 in his pocket, a new suit on his back and a lecture from the warden in his memory, Malcolm walked out of prison a free man. He did not turn around to look as he left, and he would never be inside prison as an inmate again.

In Chicago the aging Muslim leader Elijah Muhammad received the news that one of his prison converts, a Michigan native named Malcolm Little, had been released. Muhammad smiled and told one of his ministers he remembered the letters Malcolm had sent him and was looking forward to meeting him. In a few years he would realize how fateful that first meeting was to be.

"**F**REEDOM." Malcolm was sitting in a bus station, waiting for the bus that would take him home after six long years, and he said the word out loud. Until the prison system had taken all his freedoms away from him he had never realized how valuable his rights as an American citizen were. But in prison he learned what it was like to be totally ruled by someone else. His special project while in prison had been to learn as much as he could about the freedoms guaranteed under the Constitution of the United States. And now that he was finally out of jail he intended to use his knowledge in order to be a truly free man, much more free than he had been in New York or Boston. "I'm going to be as free as—"

and there he paused, wondering how to finish the sentence. Then he smiled and said aloud what he was thinking, "—a white man!"

The Malcolm Little paroled in 1952 was a much different person from the brash, strong-willed hipster society had placed behind bars in 1946. As he left prison Malcolm was sure no one had ever taken advantage of his years behind bars as he had. He had used the time to gain an education, quit using drugs and, perhaps most important, find a constructive path to follow. That path was the Muslim movement, and the guiding light was the word of Elijah Muhammad. Malcolm really had no idea where the path led but was determined to follow it as long as he possibly could. It was with this determination that he boarded the bus and headed for Detroit.

There were many reasons to return to the "Motor City." Although Malcolm had studied the Muslim movement carefully during his years behind bars, there was still much to learn before he could be accepted into the movement. His family had offered to give him that instruction as well as get him a job and a place to live. At this time Malcolm's brother Wilfred was managing a furniture store in the Detroit ghetto, and he arranged for Malcolm to be hired as a salesman. It took Malcolm only a few weeks to get to hate that job.

The furniture store was typical of white-owned stores in black communities across the nation. The store itself was managed by blacks, and only rarely would the white owners show up. The merchandise sold was overpriced and poorly made, but because the store offered "Easy Credit Payments" it did a good business. Black people, unable to get credit at other stores, would come in to buy furniture and agree to sign "the paper" that explained the easy credit system.

The one thing it really wasn't was *easy*. What the store never told its customers was that they were paying very high interest rates on the money they owed. Furniture advertised for $200, for example, would end up costing twice that much before the "easy payments" were completed. Worse, if a family missed a single payment, the store would come to claim the furniture and put it back in the store to be sold over again. It is easy to see why, when ghetto blacks rioted in the middle 1960s, stores like this were their very first target.

Malcolm did his best to put the job out of his mind. As far as he was concerned it was a way of filling the daylight hours until he could return to Wilfred's house for more Muslim instruction. He learned all the Muslim prayers and ceremonies, as well as the meaning of each. And he studied the religious history. By the time he got out of prison, he learned, the Muslim movement was small but firmly established in Chicago and Detroit. But to his utter amazement Malcolm discovered that there were over 725 million Muslims throughout the world, although most practiced a different type of religion from the Chicago and Detroit blacks. "With all those Muslims," Malcolm asked Detroit Minister Lemuel Hassan, "why are there empty seats in Detroit Temple Number One?" All Hassan could do was shrug his shoulders. For Malcolm that was not a good enough answer.

"Listen to me," he told Hassan, "I know the people on the streets. They have to be led in here by the hand. We can't just sit here and let them come to us, because they never will."

"Be patient, Malcolm," Hassan told him. "Allah will show them the way." Malcolm said he would be patient, but he assured himself that even Allah would never turn down a helping hand.

The weeks, filled with instruction, passed quickly for Malcolm. But when Hassan told the Detroit group that a car caravan would be going to Chicago to hear Elijah Muhammad speak on Labor Day, the days began dragging. Each seemed ten years long. Malcolm just couldn't wait. Finally, the big day came.

Chicago Temple Number One was quite different from the Detroit Temple. It was bigger and decorated much more lavishly. Malcolm sat nervously in the middle of the worshippers waiting for the service to begin. Then, before Malcolm realized it, Elijah Muhammad walked up to the speaker's platform and gave the traditional Muslim greeting. After all these years, Malcolm was finally seeing Elijah Muhammad in person. It was a day he would never forget.

Muhammad began his sermon that day by telling his listeners how he himself had been punished by the white man for committing the crime of being born black. "I spent three and one-half years in the federal penitentiary, and also over a year in the city jail for teaching the truth about the white man," he said. He completed the sermon by calling the white man "that devil," and said the black man could never rest until freed from the white man's power. Then he stopped and took a long drink of water.

"We have with us today," he began again, "some brothers and sisters from the Detroit Temple." And then he totally startled Malcolm by mentioning him by name. Muhammad went on to tell the story of Malcolm's daily letters.

"They were crudely written at first, but once Brother Malcolm discovered the power of Allah there was steady improvement. But," Muhammad continued, "it is now that Brother Malcolm must face the true test. Will he listen to the devil and return to his old ways of drinking, using narcotics, using women, and turning to crime? Or will he be strong enough to remain faithful?" In his mind Malcolm accepted the challenge.

That night Muhammad invited certain members of the Detroit group, including Malcolm and his family, to his home for dinner. All during the happy meal Malcolm sat silently, almost afraid to say a word. When he did manage to get up enough courage to say something, he blurted out the first thing that came to mind. "Sir," he said, "how many Muslims should there be at our Detroit services?"

"There should be thousands," Muhammad answered, "thousands."

"And how should we get them there?" Malcolm asked.

"Go after the young people," was the reply. "Once you get them, the older ones will follow through shame." Malcolm sat back with a big smile on his face and began making plans for a recruiting drive.

The meeting turned out to have a much more important result. Soon after he returned to Detroit, Malcolm received official notice that his application had been accepted and he was now a full-fledged Muslim. In the future, he was told, he would never use his slave name of Little but from that day on would be known as Malcolm X.

Malcolm X threw himself into recruiting new members for the Detroit Temple. Observing his enthusiasm, there was little Minister Hassan could do but encourage him and offer assistance whenever he could. But Malcolm's personal drive for new members did not go as well as he had thought it would. Malcolm found he was competing for the attention of Detroit blacks with many other storefront "religions," all of which made the same promises of a new, better life. There was little Malcolm could say that many, many other people before him had not said. It was only his continued devotion to "getting out on the streets with the people" that kept a steady trickle of new faces coming in for services. The membership did not increase quickly or greatly, but it did increase steadily. Eventually Malcolm's hard work would pay off and the total Detroit membership would be tripled, but for the present Malcolm felt frustrated.

At about this time Malcolm realized what was at the end of the path for him. His unhappiness at the furniture store led to his quitting and taking a series of other jobs, none of which satisfied him. It seemed that the only time he felt satisfied and fulfilled was when he was doing Muslim work. There must be a way, he said to himself, that I can spend more time doing Muslim work. There must be some way!

It was at this point that Minister Hassan asked Malcolm if he would like to address the congregation at the following Sunday's meeting. Malcolm readily agreed. In later years, when he thought back on the invitation, Malcolm would state his belief that Allah must have put the thought in Hassan's mind—when Allah thought Malcolm was ready to take this important step. Although very nervous, Malcolm delivered a sermon typical of his later speeches.

"My Brothers and Sisters," he began, "our white slavemasters' Christian religion has taught us black people here in the wilderness of North America that we will sprout wings when we die and fly up into the sky, where God will have for us a special place called heaven. This is white man's Christian religion used to brainwash us black people. And we have accepted it! We have embraced it! We have believed it! We have believed it! We have practiced it! And while we were doing all of that, for himself this blue-eyed devil has twisted his Christianity—to keep his foot on our backs . . . to keep our eyes fixed on the pie in the sky and heaven thereafter . . . while he enjoys his heaven right here . . . on earth . . . in this life!"

As the weeks passed, Malcolm became a regular speaker at Sunday meetings. Within six months, in the summer of 1953, Muhammad appointed him Assistant Minister of Detroit Temple Number One. Although he still kept his regular job, the appointment meant that Malcolm could officially devote all his free time to the Temple.

All the energy that had gone into crime in earlier years, all the energy that had been spent in the prison library during his years behind bars—all the energy he could summon—went into his new job. He would be out on the streets from the moment he got home from work until late at night. "When you sit down on that furniture you bought and it breaks," he would say, "remember the white man that sold it to you took your money and moved far, far away."

He became a familiar figure in the black neighborhoods of Detroit, and more than once he heard a local hustler tell him, "Not tonight, Malcolm; we've had enough of your preaching for a while."

But Malcolm never considered slowing down. "We didn't land on Plymouth Rock, my brothers and sisters," he was fond of saying, "Plymouth Rock landed on us!" People were usually fascinated by this smooth-talking, light-skinned black man who dared preach that hating the white man was the right and proper thing for a black man to do. "The white man *is* the devil; they are one and the same," he would say over and over, and eventually more and more people began paying attention. The membership continued growing.

Every time Malcolm could get away from his regular job he would go to Chicago and stay with Elijah Muhammad. A strong bond, almost a father-son relationship, developed between the two. "I had only one feeling about the Honorable Elijah Muhammad at this time," Malcolm would say later. "I worshipped the ground he walked on."

During these visits to Chicago Muhammad would tell Malcolm the "true" story of his life. Just as Malcolm had been taught, Muhammad had been one of the disciples of W. D. Fard and had taken charge of the Detroit-based movement after Fard disappeared. Because others had tried to take over from Muhammad, he had been forced to flee to Chicago, where he had organized Chicago Temple One. In 1942 he was arrested by the "white devil" and charged with being a draft dodger, though at that point he claimed to be 45 years old and thus ineligible for the draft. He had been sentenced to five years in jail and had served three-and-a-half before being paroled in 1946. Then he had returned to Chicago and reclaimed his place as head of the Nation of Islam. None of the stories he told Malcolm did anything to lessen the esteem Malcolm held for his spiritual leader.

The feeling must have been mutual, because Elijah Muhammad finally decided Malcolm should have a Temple of his own. He asked Malcolm if he would move to Boston and attempt to set up a Muslim Temple there. Malcolm agreed.

Each Sunday night in Boston a small group would meet in the home of one of that city's small Muslim population. The group included all the people Malcolm had been able to persuade to come and listen, as well as a few of his friends from the old days. Malcolm would tell them about the physical slavery of the black man in early America and explain that the chains were still there, but that now they were the chains of mental slavery. "Free!" he would laugh sarcastically. "The black man is not free. He is only as free as the white man gives him permission to be." And out of each group a few would come forward when Malcolm asked, "Who will follow the Honorable Elijah Muhammad?" The next Sunday the new members would return with some of their friends, and in this way the Boston Muslim group grew until it was large enough to afford the rent of a storefront to use as a Temple.

Although his time in Boston was limited, Malcolm made it a point to seek out his old friends. Shorty had gotten out of prison about the same time Malcolm had and, just like Malcolm, had taken advantage of his time behind bars. He had studied music there and now had a little band of his own. When Malcolm surprised him, the two had a great reunion, but a wall appeared between them when Malcolm began talking about his new-found religion. "Not me," Shorty told him, "not me," and the two friends parted, still on good terms. The Temple, Muslim Temple Number 11, was opened in March, 1954.

At this point the goal of the Muslim movement was simple: full rights and full equality for the black man. The message being spread by Muslim ministers was clear: the white man, the devil, had long been keeping the black man in chains. The black man was actually superior to the white man and had to reclaim his place. Although little mention was made of it at this point, the message was clear for members of the Muslim movement that when it became necessary, and when all other paths were blocked, blacks must take up arms to gain the proverbial "eye for an eye."

At this time in our nation's history other black groups were moving along different paths. For over 150 years blacks had been looking to the American court system for relief from their status as second-class citizens. In most instances the courts had failed them. But in 1948 and again in 1950 the courts changed direction. Two important cases marked a turning of the tide. The Supreme Court ruled in *Sipuel v. Board of Regents* and *Sweatt v. Painter* that, although separate but equal schools were permissible, when the black schools were not as good as the white schools blacks had to be admitted to the white schools.

The major "civil rights" case occurred in 1954. In *Brown v. the Board of Education of Topeka, Kansas,* the court ruled that separate schools could never really be equal and that calling them equal did not make them so. That court ruled that all schools in the nation had to be integrated. But making a ruling and carrying it out were two different things. Although all-white schools were seemingly outlawed in 1954, fifteen years later integration was not yet an accomplished fact.

But now the lines had been drawn, with Muslims teaching white hatred and separation of the races on one side, and the Supreme Court upholding the Constitution on the other. All that was needed was a spokesman for the third side, the side that maintained blacks and whites could live together in peace and harmony. About a year after the Brown decision, one emerged.

On December 1st, 1955 Rosa Parks of Montgomery, Alabama, got on a bus. She had had a long day at work and was tired, so she took the first seat she saw. It turned out to be in the front of the bus, an area Negroes were forbidden by law to sit in! The law stated quite clearly that blacks must either sit in the back of the bus or stand up. When the driver asked Rosa Parks to get up, she look up at him wearily and said no. She was quickly arrested.

Word spread through the black community. A group of Negro leaders met that evening to lay out a plan. Since seventy-five percent of the people who used the bus were black, they reasoned, the bus system could not survive without black passengers. Until the law was changed, they decided, no black people would use the bus system. The committee decided to give the responsibility for organizing the boycott to a young local Baptist Minister named Martin Luther King.

The results are history. After the successful boycott entered its third month, King and other black leaders were arrested and charged with conducting an illegal economic boycott. The case went into court, and as they had done recently in most cases, the courts ruled in favor of the blacks. Segregating buses, the courts said, was illegal, and they ruled that any person could sit anywhere he wished on public transportation. But the boycott had a much more lasting effect. It marked the first time Americans had heard of Martin Luther King, the man who was to lead the major opposition to Muslim thinking for the next ten years, and the man who was to meet tragic death the same way Malcolm did, at the hands of a gun-bearing assassin.

While all this was happening in the South, Malcolm kept himself quite busy. After the Boston Temple was established he was sent to Philadelphia. The words came more naturally now. "The Christian world has failed to give the black man justice," he would tell listeners. "The American government has failed to give her twenty million ex-slaves payment for three hundred years of free slave labor. We have been America's most faithful servants during peacetime and her bravest soldiers during wartime. But still white Christians have been unwilling to accept us as fellow human beings. So the black man must turn away from white churches and toward the Nation of Islam." Recruiting in Philadelphia went more quickly than it had in Boston. In a matter of months Malcolm was able to tell Muhammad that Temple Number Twelve in Philadelphia was an established fact.

Malcolm was called back to Chicago for his next assignment. He had no idea what it would be when he sat down with Elijah Muhammad. He had done very well in Boston and Philadelphia, Muhammad told him, and he was being carefully watched. He showed great promise, and the people of the streets seemed to respond to him. It was time for Malcolm to take the big step, Muhammad continued. Then he paused and asked in a low voice, "Are you ready to go back to New York?"

New York. Malcolm didn't know how to react to that magic name. Once it had meant the beginning and end of everything important to him. But now? Now he wasn't sure. Could he survive in New York? Could he resist the temptations? Then he thought, "How selfish I am." Here he was, thinking about himself, when there were millions of black people who had never even heard of the Muslims. It should be simple to start a Temple there, Malcolm thought, and as soon as he began thinking in terms of bringing the Nation of Islam to New York a calm came over him. He knew Allah was telling him to go to New York; he would have no problems.

"I would be very happy to return to New York," he said.

ARLEM had changed in the years Malcolm had been away. The Harlem Malcolm had known had been a group of immigrant communities, with the black section only a part of the entire area. Drug traffic had existed on a relatively small level and in most cases really didn't involve the working-class black man or his children. That had all changed. The large Italian community in East Harlem had almost totally disappeared, taking with it most of the white people of Harlem. With the exception of the newest group of immigrants, the Puerto Ricans, Harlem was now almost totally black. And drugs had become the major community problem.

Malcolm couldn't walk half a block without either being approached by someone selling marijuana or "hard" drugs, or seeing a youngster obviously under the influence of dope. Malcolm was seeing Harlem through different eyes than he had nine years ago, and he didn't like what he saw.

Physically there had been little change in the neighborhood. The buildings were nine years older and dirtier and there were more broken windows, but the lights still burned the brightest, the buildings were still the tallest and the streets still the noisiest. The change was in the people. There was a feeling of fear in the air that Malcolm didn't recognize. The friendliness of the community was gone. The people kept more to themselves. Within a few weeks Malcolm realized the extent of the drug problem in Harlem and understood the fear: the people were worried about their children. From the number of addicts Malcolm saw on the street he realized that they had good reason. "If only they knew what they were doing to themselves," Malcolm said to himself. "If they only knew."

Malcolm began spending much of his time dealing with the drug problem and was not surprised to discover that the Harlem drug trade was almost totally white-controlled. "Just another example of white people killing black people," he would say.

The grapevine spread the word of Malcolm's return quickly, and all over Harlem conversations were almost the same. "Guess what," someone would say, "Detroit Red is back in town."

"Detroit Red? You're kidding," would be the reply.

"And listen to this. His conk is gone and he's become a preacher!"

"A preacher? Detroit Red? That must be his new hustle."

But when they saw him in his short haircut and neatly pressed suit they knew the change had been for real. Detroit Red was indeed back in town, but it was a changed Red. For starters he let it be known that his name was Malcolm X and that was what he expected to be called. "There is no Detroit Red any longer," he said. And he set out to locate two people, West Indian Archie and Sammy the Pimp.

The grapevine brought the information in a single afternoon. Sammy was dead, a victim of his own success. He had gone into the numbers racket in a big way and been very successful. In fact, he had been too successful for someone's liking, and the police had found him lying across his bed, money spread all over the room. It paid for a handsome funeral.

West Indian Archie was tougher to find. When Malcolm finally tracked down the man who had once given him twenty-four hours to get out of Harlem or pay his debt, he found a shell of the hustler he had known. Archie was old and sick and, Malcolm thought sadly, just waiting to die. When Archie opened the front door of his one-room apartment and saw Malcolm standing there, he didn't react at all. Then, all at once, he realized who it was that was staring back at him. "Red," he said in a calm voice, "it's really awfully nice to see you." The two had a long conversation, making their peace over the still-remembered incident, and then Malcolm said goodbye.

As he was walking down the stairs, one thought stayed in his mind: "So this is how it ends for the hustlers." The men he saw sleeping in doorways and begging for a few pennies made him shudder. If Allah had not found me, he thought, this would have been how I ended up. All praise is due Allah!

After seeing to it that word of his return was passed around, Malcolm threw himself into his work. The Muslim group in New York was so small that their "Temple" consisted only of a small storefront, and even that was rarely more than half full. The entire movement, in fact, was almost totally unknown throughout Harlem. Malcolm set his first goal: to gain some attention for the Nation of Islam.

If recruiting had been tough in Boston and Philadelphia, that was nothing compared with the problem of gaining members in New York. Malcolm just couldn't understand it. With literally millions of blacks in New York why was it so tough to recruit a few hundred for his cause? A few hundred? In those days Malcolm would have settled gladly for fifty or sixty. He realized that publicity was the important thing, so he organized the few members he had into a group to hand out pamphlets. "Come hear about the devil white man who has enslaved you," they read. But new faces were seldom seen, and Malcolm just could not figure out why.

One Sunday morning, as he stood watching the thousands of black people streaming out of the Christian churches and other storefront churches, the answer came to him. The Muslims were religious newcomers in the community. Everyone already had a place to go on Sunday mornings. Malcolm had a ready answer—Sunday afternoons. So the Muslims scheduled services for two o'clock in the afternoon and spent the mornings "fishing." As the blacks came out of their churches Sunday morning, Muslims would be there with pamphlets, shouting, "Black people, now that you've heard the white man's version, come to our black church this afternoon and hear the black man's version." People did come, and when they got there Malcolm gave a sermon. They were never disappointed.

"Moses was raised up among the enslaved people at a time when God was planning to restore them to a land of their own," Malcolm would cry in a loud voice, "where they could give birth to a new civilization, completely independent of their new slavemasters. Pharaoh opposed God's plan and God's servant, so Pharoah and his people were destroyed.

"Jesus was sent among his people at a time when God was planning to bring another great change. The forgiveness preached by Jesus two thousand years ago ushered in a new type of civilization, the Christian civilization.

"The Holy Prophet Muhammad came six hundred years after Jesus with another message that did not destroy Christianity but put a dent in it. Now, today, God has sent Elijah Muhammad among the downtrodden and oppressed so-called American Negroes to warn that God is again preparing to bring about another great change, only this time it will be a final change. Mr. Muhammad teaches that the religion of Islam is the only solution to the problems that confront our people here in America."

The people who came listened to Malcolm carefully and understood exactly what he was talking about. Many of them began making it a weekly habit to go to their regular Sunday services and then walk over to Malcolm's storefront to hear "the new preacher." But when the time came to come forward and join the Muslims, very few took the big step. Malcolm quickly discovered the reason: the very strict moral code of the Muslims scared a lot of potential members away. This code included everything from not drinking, gambling, cursing or dating to not going to the movies or even to sports events. Only the truly dedicated could live by such harsh rules. But if the nation of Islam was to survive, such a strict code was a necessity.

Often Malcolm would use the time reserved for his sermons to try to explain the reasons for the moral code. "The white man has put you where you are," he would say, "and it is the white man that makes it impossible for you to find a decent place to live. It is the white man that makes it impossible for you to get a good job. It is the white man that charges you high prices so you can't save any money. And it is the white man that wants you to stay immoral, unclean and ignorant. As long as we stay that way the white man will always say, 'See, they can't even take care of themselves,' and he will control us. We can never win our freedom and justice until we are doing things for ourselves." Harlemites listened and agreed, but the growing process was still a slow and painful one for Malcolm.

Muhammad had long ago realized that Malcolm had something that made people listen to him and believe him, and he called it charisma. He was determined to take advantage of this quality. While New York business kept Malcolm in the city over the weekend, during the week Muhammad would have Malcolm traveling up and down the East Coast. Malcolm helped to organize and set up Temple Thirteen in Springfield, Massachusetts, and Temple Fourteen in Hartford, Connecticut. Temple Fifteen, with Malcolm's help, opened in Atlanta, Georgia. Malcolm was so busy traveling back and forth between Muslim groups, "fishing" for new recruits, setting up classes for Muslim men and women, and helping run established Temples, that he had absolutely no time for his own personal life. Not that he missed it. He thrived on Muslim activities. And the most important thing in his life, the Nation of Islam, was indeed beginning to show signs of great expansion by the end of 1955.

Setting up a Temple was easy compared with the day-to-day running of one. Once a Temple was established it had to provide for the needs of all its members, and that meant an activity just about every night of the week. Monday night, for example, the Fruit of Islam trained. The FOI learned the military arts of judo and karate, training that would help them protect Muslim Temples and members, as well as studying current events, health subjects and manners . . . everything necessary to become a complete male.

Tuesday night was Unity Night. Muslim men and women would gather in the Temple to share some light refreshments and each others' company. This was the "social night" of the Temple. Wednesdays were reserved for Student Enrollment, where the basic ideas behind the Muslim movement were taught and discussed.

Muslim Girls' Training and General Civilization classes were held Thursday nights. This was the women's equivalent of Monday nights. The women learned the arts of keeping a Muslim home and raising children in the movement. Civilization was also taught Friday night. Muslim men and women were taught how to live together with understanding and respect. Saturday night was the only open night, but most often a group of Muslims would gather at someone's home for an evening of fun and discussions. Sunday services started the whole cycle all over again.

It was at one of the Thursday meetings that a pretty

young Muslim teacher caught Malcolm's eye. Since the day he had left for prison Malcolm had attempted to keep women out of his thoughts. He felt he had too many important things to accomplish. There simply was no time for women. But there was something different about this teacher. He couldn't explain exactly what it was, but somehow she attracted him in a way no woman had for nine years. The subjects she taught were hygiene and medical facts, and she taught these subjects from information gained while spending her days in nursing school at one of New York's largest hospitals. Her name was Sister Betty X.

Although he certainly did not intend to, Malcolm found himself thinking more and more about Sister Betty X. "That's a pretty fine girl," he would hear himself thinking, and another voice in his mind would answer, "But you don't have time for girls now." Malcolm began to feel like a young schoolboy with his first crush. He made it a point to stop in at almost all of her lectures, and he would find himself planning to bump into her "accidentally" on social evenings.

Although he wanted to get to know this girl better, the Muslim social code, which he strictly followed, had a rule against dating. He came up with a solution. He would solve his problem and help the movement at the same time. Since she was a teacher, she certainly should have as much knowledge in her field as possible. With that in mind he invited her to attend an exhibit at the Museum of Natural History. She said she would love to go.

Malcolm was nervous as he dressed for his first "date" since before he was sent to prison. "It's just another job," he tried to tell himself, "and I'm just doing my best to help this sister improve herself as an instructor." Of course, even he didn't believe this little lie. All through their afternoon together strange new thoughts kept running through his mind: "How would it affect the Nation of Islam if I married this girl?" "But she is the right height for a man as tall as I am." "And how do I know she even likes me?" "Well, isn't Muhammad himself married?" "It's my duty to help increase the number of Muslim families in the country, to set an example." For all practical purposes Malcolm decided that afternoon that he would eventually ask Sister Betty X to marry him.

"Eventually," he kept telling himself. "I'm just not ready yet." But that other voice inside him kept saying, "Okay, when?" and he just didn't have an answer. In the meantime, during one of his frequent trips to Chicago he had informed Elijah Muhammad that he was considering a very "serious step." Muhammad just smiled and nodded.

"And who is she?" he asked.

Malcolm's mouth flew open. He didn't realize he had done such a poor job of disguising his feelings. He answered, "A sister from New York."

"I'd like very much to meet her," Muhammad said, and it was soon arranged for Sister Betty X to come to Chicago. The recent success of the Muslims had made it possible for sisters from different Temples to come to Chicago to meet Muhammad, and Betty was offered one of these trips. After she left, Muhammad spoke to Malcolm. "About this Sister Betty X," he said, "I've met her and spoken to her." He paused and Malcolm waited. "And I think she's a wonderful girl."

"Eventually," one voice said; and the other answered, "Now." Finally "now" won out. Malcolm was traveling to Detroit to visit his family for the first time in many years. Wilfred had recently been made Minister of the Detroit Temple and Malcolm was driving out to offer belated congratulations. During the whole long drive he argued the question of marriage with himself.

The answer finally came as he pulled into a gas station. "Oh, why not?" he thought and went into a pay phone and dialed Betty in New York. He didn't hesitate for a second when she picked up the phone. "Look," he said in what must be one of the most direct marriage proposals in history, "do you want to get married?"

There was silence on the other end.

Oh, great! Malcolm thought: Now you've done it. Now she'll tell all of the others what a big fool she made out of Brother Malcolm.

He was wrong. "Yes," she said simply.

"We don't have much time, then, so you'd better get right on a plane and get out to Detroit."

This was on Monday. The next morning, Malcolm and Betty drove to Lansing, Michigan, raced around town all day getting the proper blood tests and certificates, and were married by a white Justice of the Peace in the afternoon. There, Malcolm told himself, now you've gone and done it. And he settled down to married life.

It didn't take Betty long to realize that she came second to recruiting new Muslim members. Although the movement was growing slowly, it was indeed growing. One of the biggest surprises of Malcolm's life occurred during one of his recruitment sermons in Boston. After he had finished speaking he asked, "Now who will come forward and follow the word of Elijah Muhammad?" From the back of the room a woman rose and came forward. It was Ella! Malcolm practically burst with pride.

Attendance in Philadelphia was up. Attendance in Hartford was up, and with the exception of New York, all the Temples seemed to be doing well. Malcolm had tried every method he could think of to make the New York Temple the leader in the East, but nothing seemed to work. With all the other storefront Churches competing for membership the Muslims failed to attract the attention of the Harlem community. What was needed, Malcolm realized, was a dramatic example of the growing power of the Muslims. But what kind of example?

The answer came one cold night. Two white policemen patrolling in Harlem stopped to break up a fight. After separating the brawlers they told the crowd to go home. With the exception of two Muslim bystanders, the people left. The policemen then started hitting the Muslims with their nightsticks, opening a severe gash in one's scalp. Then they took him to the stationhouse. The other Muslim called a Muslim-operated restaurant, and within an hour fifty members of the Fruit of Islam showed up outside the restaurant. They marched in ranks to the police station and stood at rigid attention in front. The word quickly spread throughout Harlem: "The Muslims are ready to fight the cops outside the police station."

"What are the Muslims?" was the usual reply, but from every corner of Harlem the curious came to see what was happening.

As soon as he received word of what was happening Malcolm raced to the scene. When he arrived, the Fruit of Islam had already taken their positions. There was no doubt in anyone's mind, Malcolm's or the policemen's inside, that the FOI would attack the station if the word was given. And Malcolm would be the one to give it. The first thing he did was demand to see the beaten Brother.

"He's not here," one of the policemen answered.

Malcolm remembered his sense of the dramatic. He walked to the window and looked out at the gathering crowd. "If *WE* don't see our Brother, there's no telling what a crowd this size might do."

Finally the police admitted that the Muslim was there but told Malcolm he would not be permitted to see him. Malcolm said that was fine with him, but what about all those Muslims outside, who had sworn not to move until they had seen their Brother? The police really had no choice; they took Malcolm into the cellroom.

Malcolm could hardly believe what he saw. The Brother, Johnson Hinton, was lying there with blood all over his face. He was only semiconscious. Malcolm demanded that the police call for an ambulance and have Hinton taken to a hospital. The police agreed, and within minutes Hinton was on his way to Harlem Hospital. In small groups the Muslims walked the long blocks to the hospital, followed by onlookers.

When Doctors at Harlem Hospital told Malcolm that Hinton was being operated on and would be given the best possible care, Malcolm gave the word for the Muslims to return to their homes. But the point had been made. Harlem was now well aware that the Muslims existed. The Harlem demonstration had shown the community that a tightly unified, proud, self-reliant group could succeed. The word "Muslim" began to meet with instant recognition. Attendance grew rapidly now. Young people in particular were attracted to the movement, and as Muhammad had predicted, once the young began showing up, the older ones followed. Soon the New York Temple was growing just as fast as Malcolm had hoped.

As for Hinton, Doctors had to put a steel plate in his head, and when he finally got out of the hospital he sued New York City, charging police brutality. He was awarded $70,000.

But Malcolm's vision extended much further than New York. The time was ripe for great expansion, and events that had been months in the making would make the expansion possible.

eight | *The Black Muslims*

ALCOM'S status within the Muslim movement continued to grow. Whenever a new Temple was
being organized Malcolm was sure to be there to lend
support. Whenever an already established Temple had a
recruiting drive Malcolm was usually among its leaders.
His dedication to the Muslims did not go unnoticed. In
the black community, where the movement was gaining
many new members and much attention, the name Malcolm X was becoming well known.

But the Nation of Islam was almost totally unknown
among whites. As far as most white Americans were
concerned, the "civil-rights movement" consisted of in-

tegrating high schools and passing impressive-sounding bills. But in 1958 blacks, led by Martin Luther King, took the offensive and the famed "sit-ins" began.

A group of black youths would walk into a store that refused to serve food to blacks, and sit down. They would refuse to move when asked, and when the police came, they would let themselves be arrested.

Their places at the food counters would be taken by other blacks until, because the store was losing too much money, the management began serving food to blacks.

A black comedian told an audience he walked into one of these stores and sat down. When the waitress said, "I'm sorry, but we don't serve Negroes," he looked her right in the eye and answered, "That's fine, because I don't eat them!"

The sit-ins soon became kneel-ins at all-white churches, wade-ins at all-white beaches, and even read-ins at segrated libraries.

Having to meet the challenge of this more moderate branch, Malcolm and the Muslims started to urge specific policies. "The American black," Malcolm said, "should be focusing his every effort toward building his *own* businesses and decent homes for himself. As other ethnic groups have done, let the black people, wherever possible, however possible, patronize their own kind, and start in that way to build up the black race's ability to do for itself." The Muslims started their own "Buy-Black" campaign, setting up as many Muslim-owned and Muslim-operated businesses as possible.

Within the black community the two lines were clearly drawn. If they were to take part in the movement, blacks had to make a choice: They could follow the path of Martin Luther King and work toward a day when blacks and whites could live together peacefully. Or they could choose that of the Muslims, which said that white people would never accept blacks and thus the only answer was complete and total separation of the races.

Lawyer Thurgood Marshall, later to become the first black man to sit on the United States Supreme Court, was one of the more moderate leaders who spoke out against the Muslims. "The Muslims," he said, "are run by a bunch of thugs originally from prisons and jails and financed, I am sure, by some Arab group."

Malcolm fought back verbally. "The followers of Martin Luther King," he said, "will cut each other from head to foot, but they will not do anything to defend themselves against the attacks of the white man. King is the best weapon of the white man . . . when the white man wants to attack Negroes they can't defend themselves because of this foolish philosophy—you're not supposed to fight and you're not supposed to defend yourself.

"We don't advocate violence, but Mr. Muhammad does teach that any human being who is intelligent has a right to defend himself. We do not start trouble, but we do not turn the other cheek. And you need someone who is going to fight. You don't need any kneeling-in or crawling-in."

In 1959 the Muslim movement, well known throughout every black ghetto, entered a new era. Mike Wallace, a white television interviewer, persuaded the Muslims to let him do a documentary about the movement. The show, many months in production, was called "The Hate that Hate Produced." It was intended to inform white people about the Nation of Islam, and it did. Here, for the first time, white people all over America were seeing and hearing about a black group that actually preached hatred of the white men!

Newspaper stories followed the television program, and then national magazines began to do stories on the Muslims. In a matter of a few months the movement had become well known throughout the country and every day received more publicity—most of it bad. The Muslims were called "hate-dealers," "black racists," "Communist-inspired," and almost anything else editors could think of. The net result was the creation of a great deal of outrage and fear in the white community, new interest in the movement in the black community, and national attention and publicity for Elijah Muhammad and his chief spokesman, Malcolm X.

At about the time "Hate" was being shown to a nationwide audience, a noted black historian, C. Eric Lincoln, chose the Nation of Islam as the subject of his doctoral thesis, a lengthy paper required of those attempting to obtain Ph.D. degrees. The idea for this paper came from a report turned in by one of Lincoln's students in a high school religion class he taught. Lincoln's thesis eventually became a book, *The Black Muslims in America,* and gained even more attention for the movement. Furthermore, the American press took the phrase "Black Muslims" from its title and began referring to the Nation of Islam as the Black Muslim movement. The American public quickly accepted the phrase and adopted it for everyday use.

Malcolm's phone never stopped ringing. Because Muhammad had, for all practical purposes, made Malcolm his national spokesman, every type of request came to him—make a speech here, appear on a television or radio show, write an article for a magazine, or be interviewed by this or that publication. Malcolm had become a national figure. He accepted as many of the invitations as he could, always spreading the Muslim word. Stories about him appeared in *Life, Look, Newsweek* and *Time,* the four major weekly magazines in America. Newspapers from nations all over the globe picked up the story of this American Muslim group and printed it.

The movement was becoming known world-wide but, as Malcolm feared, it was also being misunderstood, particularly among the whites. In order to try to correct any false ideas people might have, Malcolm wrote an introduction for himself that he used whenever he appeared.

"I am Malcolm X," he would begin. "I represent Elijah Muhammad, the spiritual head of the fastest-growing group of Muslims in the Western Hemisphere. We who follow him know that he has been divinely taught and sent to us by God himself. We believe that the miserable plight of America's twenty million black people is the fulfillment of a divine prophecy. We also believe the presence today in America of the Honorable Elijah Muhammad, his teachings among so-called Negroes, and his naked warning to America concerning her treatment of these so-called Negroes is all the fulfillment of divine prophecy."

Moments alone, or time to spend with his wife and new daughter, came rarely for Malcolm, but when they did he would take the time to relax and gather his thoughts. The publicity, over-all, had been wonderful for the movement. It had given the Muslims respectability among the blacks who had been hesitant about joining. Whenever Elijah Muhammad spoke now, huge crowds would gather to hear him. Over ten thousand people came to the famed St. Nicholas Arena in New York City when Muhammad spoke there. The Detroit Temple, which once had been able to muster only ten busloads for a trip to Chicago, now sent ten times that amount for the Chicago meetings. And most important to Malcolm was the fact that these were black-only meetings; no whites at all were permitted. The Muslims were giving the black man his due respect.

Malcolm would always speak at the major Muslim meetings. Before introducing Elijah Muhammad, he would tell the audience, "The Honorable Elijah Muhammad is the first black leader among us with the courage to tell us something which, when you begin to think of it back in your homes, you will realize black people have been living with—which we have been seeing, we have been suffering, all of our lives. Our enemy is the white man!"

Malcolm's life was a continuous whirl of traveling and talking, traveling and talking. When he did pause for a moment, one thought filled his mind: how lucky he had been to find Allah, who had taken him from a prison cell in Massachusetts to world-wide renown, who had given him a wife and daughter, and—most important—had enabled him to do something worthwhile for black people. Malcolm was indeed satisfied with the way things had been going, but he would never really be content until the Muslim dream of black separation was achieved.

When Elijah Muhammad spoke and said, "So let us separate from this white man, and for the same reason he gives, in time to save ourselves from any more integration," he was just saying out loud what Malcolm was thinking. The Muslim plan for black-white separation was no secret; it had been well publicized in the press— a piece of land in this country where black people could establish a black state and where they could live by themselves.

The Muslims demanded payment from the Government for all the free black labor given to America during the days of slavery. Malcolm echoed these demands in his speeches. "Integration is not good for either side. It will destroy your [white] race, and your government knows it will destroy ours and the problem will remain unsolved. God has declared that these twenty million ex-slaves must have a home of their own. After four hundred years here among the whites, we are absolutely convinced we can never live together in peace, unless we are willing to remain slaves to our former masters. Therefore immediate and complete separation is the only solution."

Although Malcolm had no real free time of his own, he managed to write a weekly column in Harlem's famed newspaper, *The Amsterdam News*. When he saw how widespread his readership was, he did just as Marcus Garvey had done before him—founded a newspaper. *Muhammad Speaks* became the official publication of the Muslim movement. All the publicity had brought in many new members, and the new members brought in one very necessary item—money. For the first time the Muslims had enough money to put some of their plans into effect, and they began to establish a Muslim business community, totally owned and operated by Muslims. The businesses were formed to show blacks that they could be independent of white help, and therefore the people who ran these businesses would only buy and sell to black people. The idea was to keep the money in the black community.

Meanwhile, speaking invitations kept pouring in.

Malcolm had become a poised, convincing speaker and totally enjoyed the challenge of facing an anti-Muslim audience. Because Muhammad was in poor health he became more and more dependent on Malcolm to deliver the Muslim message. So, in the eight years since he joined the movement Malcolm had risen to the number two spot and, as he himself looked at it, he had risen from a convict to a respected speaker.

The questions all interviewers asked were basically the same. After welcoming Malcolm they would ask him to describe briefly the "Black Muslim" movement. Following Malcolm's description, they would recite a long list of advances the moderate civil-rights movement had achieved and then ask, "Wouldn't you say that there have been great advances toward integration made by the black people in the last few years?"

This was a question for which Malcolm had a ready answer, an answer still used today by many black leaders: "For four hundred years the white man had a knife in the black man's back—and now the white man starts to take the knife out, maybe six inches, and you say the black man is supposed to be grateful. Since you put the knife there in the first place, you can say you've taken it halfway out. Since it's my back I say it's still halfway in!"

Because he now had a large personal following, whenever a major event in the civil-rights movement occurred, reporters would rush to get Malcolm's view. For example, in 1961 a group of black and white people banded together on a bus and set out to travel through the Deep South, testing new civil-rights laws. Malcolm thought these "Freedom Riders" were ridiculous. He said he knew the North quite well, and the Northern ghettos had enough rats and roaches to be killed to keep all the

Freedom Riders busy for many months. Malcolm went on to say that liberal New York City actually had more integration problems than Mississippi, and that if people really wanted to do some good they would stay home and work on the problems of their own ghettos.

Again, two years later, when 250,000 people, including 60,000 whites, participated in the famous "March On Washington" to hear Dr. King make his famous "I Have A Dream" speech, Malcolm found much to criticize. The original idea, he said, had been for blacks from all over the country to come to Washington and cause a great disturbance, demanding of Congress and the President some definite action on civil rights. But, according to Malcolm, the movement had been taken over by white people who thought the whole thing a wonderful idea. Instead of an angry black march, it was turned into an outing, a company picnic. As far as getting anything accomplished was concerned—well, Malcolm said, he had to laugh. It was a waste of time, impressive in terms of numbers but still a waste of time.

By the beginning of 1963 Malcolm had become one of the most controversial men in America. Next to Arizona Senator Barry Goldwater, the Republican nominee for the Presidency in 1964, he was the most popular college speaker in the country. Perhaps this was because Malcolm was at his best when talking to college students. "It's like being on a battlefield," he said of his college lectures, "with intellectual and philosophical bullets. It is an exciting battle of ideas."

But the single thing Malcolm never forgot was his purpose. He never let the national attention he received go to his head. "I am the representative of the Prophet Elijah Muhammad. His will is my will." Muhammad never forgot this either, and he continued to let Malcolm know he approved of everything he was doing. Their relationship continued to be close. As Malcolm once remembered, "I believed so strongly in Mr. Muhammad that I would have hurled myself between him and an assassin."

At some point the pendulum of life begins to slow down and level off. This is what started happening to Malcolm now. For the very first time, he began to hear blacks criticizing the movement. "The Muslims certainly talk tough," said a voice in Harlem, "but they never do anything unless somebody bothers Muslims." "All he ever does is talk," said a more moderate voice. "CORE and SNCC and some of them people of Dr. King's are out getting beat over the head." Even Muhammad criticized Malcolm for the first time, telling him he thought he was speaking at too many colleges.

But Malcolm could accept the objections. The Muslims—or black Muslims, as the press called them—were now firmly established. There were over 100 mosques (or Temples) throughout the nation. The very first goal had now been achieved: the Nation of Islam had been set up in America. But in what form? None of the Muslim-watchers—the press, radio and television—were able to describe accurately what the movement was. A religion, as Malcolm claimed? A political movement? Both? Neither? There were many different opinions.

The *New York Herald Tribune,* at that time one of the finest papers in the nation, could not answer the question. "The Black Muslims," the now-dead newspaper said, "are unshakable in their claims that theirs is . . . a religious movement. Those who join must sever their ties with other churches. They must agree to follow the

Moslem dietary laws against pork and alcohol. Malcolm X says the faithful eat only one meal a day and face the East to say their prayers."

Author George Breitman spoke of the Muslims as much more than a religious movement. "From a scientific standpoint, Black Muslim history is no more or no less fantastic or strange than other religions. But the Black Muslims are a movement as well as a religious group, providing a kind of haven and hope and salvation for outcasts, encouragement at self-reform and brotherhood."

Time magazine represented the other viewpoint, disbelieving the Muslims' religious claims, although they had "set up their movement with all the trappings of a religion."

Malcolm didn't have to be told what the Muslim movement was; he knew. It was simply everything—his religion and, indeed, his life. He often wondered what would have happened to him if Allah had not accepted him. He decided that without the Muslims he would probably not have survived. In fact, even now he doubted that he could live separated from the movement. He was soon to find out just how right he was.

*The Honorable Elijah Muhammad addresses a Muslim convention in the
early 1960's*

Malcolm addresses a crowd in New York early in February 1963

*Malcolm arrives in Washington, D.C. in May 1963 to set up Black Muslim
headquarters there. Muslims planned a series of Negro-only meetings to
seek solutions to the capital's crime problems.*

Malcolm X holds up a paper for the crowd to see during a Black Muslim rally in July 1963

Entering car at Kennedy Airport after his tour of the Middle East (May 1964), Malcolm carries his daughter Ilysah

Malcolm X leans on shoulder of his friend and pupil Cassius Clay (Muhammad Ali) at a soda fountain party in 1964. Clay had just beaten Sonny Liston to become the heavyweight champion of the world.

nine | *Banished*

As America soared into the sixties filled with optimism, so did the Nation of Islam. Because of the hard work of Malcolm and a few other key people, the Muslims had become the fastest growing black organization in the country. The problem had once been finding enough people to fill the storefront churches and rented halls, but now it became finding storefronts and halls large enough to fit all the people who flocked to hear Muslim words. In New York, for example, where Malcolm had had such trouble getting one Temple organized, there were now three operating.

As for Malcolm himself, he was now busier than

ever, if that was possible. Often he would spend four or five nights a week on planes traveling from campuses to television or radio interviews, to Muslim functions, and then, as often as possible, home to Betty and his growing family.

As Malcolm saw things, there was only one dark cloud on the horizon—the health of Elijah Muhammad. The Nation's leader was growing progressively weaker, and finally his doctors told him he must move to a drier climate. The Muslims purchased a house for Muhammad in Phoenix, Arizona, and Malcolm made it a practice to visit at least once a month. As far as he knew, his relationship with Muhammad was unchanged, but every once in a while he would hear a rumor that Muhammad felt differently.

"Malcolm likes the attention," one rumor went. "He likes playing the role of a Big Man!"

"Malcolm is building his own following, and Muhammad doesn't like that at all," went another.

Because he knew that none of what these people were saying was true, Malcolm didn't let the rumors bother him. He just kept going about his Muslim duties and, as always, continued to emphasize to his listeners that he was only acting as a spokesman for Elijah Muhammad.

But the rumors persisted. And other little things that took place made it look as if Malcolm was indeed beginning to lose favor with the Muslims. *Muhammad Speaks,* which was now being edited by one of Muhammad's sons, began printing less and less about Malcolm's activities. Also, Muslim officials in Chicago were considerably cooler when Malcolm had to go there on business. And the rumors about his building a personal following increased.

He searched for a reason for this change in attitude. "They couldn't possibly doubt my devotion to the Nation," Malcolm said to himself. And, as far as he could figure out, that left only one possible answer—jealousy. For months now, newspapers had been guessing who would succeed Elijah Muhammad as the Muslims' leader, and the choice seemed to have narrowed to two people, Malcolm X and Raymond Sharrieff, Muhammad's son-in-law and commander of the Fruit of Islam. Malcolm began wondering if some friends of his rival were at the bottom of this plot against him.

Malcolm decided on the strategy he would use to combat the rumors. If other Muslims were indeed jealous of all the publicity he was receiving, he would put an end to as much of it as he could. Although he felt he was hurting the Nation in doing so, Malcolm began turning down interviews and refused to appear on television shows. Whenever a photographer snapped his picture he would hand him a photograph of Muhammad and request that he use that instead. Whenever he spoke, he made a point of emphasizing his position as only one of many Muslim ministers.

But nothing seemed to help. Every time an important event took place, reporters called him for his comments. Most of the time he resisted, but when Southern black leader Medgar Evers was shot in the back and a bomb set off in a Birmingham, Alabama, church killed four little girls, Malcolm said the things he felt had to be said, no matter what those officials in Chicago thought.

All this time he kept one thought in mind: "As long as Elijah Muhammad still believes in me I can accept the challenge from the rest of them." And there was every indication that despite the rumors Muhammad did indeed still believe in Malcolm. In early 1963 he appointed Malcolm the first National Muslim Minister, saying, "This is my most faithful, hardworking Minister. He will follow me until he dies."

Muhammad proved to be wrong about that. Malcolm's faith was soon to be deeply shaken. A newspaper story in a Chicago paper reported that two former Muslim secretaries were suing Muhammad for money to support their children, claiming that he was the children's father. Malcolm's first reaction was disbelief. Muslim laws included a very strict moral code, and Muhammad himself had suspended people from the movement for doing exactly the thing he was now accused of. Malcolm vowed to get to the bottom of this and expose the people trying to ruin Elijah Muhammad's reputation. What his investigation revealed upset him even more.

As far as he could determine, the accusations were true! And in talking to these two secretaries, Malcolm discovered even more than he had bargained for. Muhammad had spent much of his time talking to these women about Malcolm. He told them that Malcolm X was the best Minister he had ever had, but that some day he would turn against the movement, so he was to be considered dangerous. Malcolm found it hard to believe that Muhammad, while praising him in public, actually distrusted him and spoke against him in private.

Malcolm was overwhelmed. He didn't know what to do, or where he could turn for help. His major worry was that news of Muhammad's conduct would get out, be printed, and destroy the Muslim movement. In order to prepare for that disaster Malcolm began changing his message when he spoke to Muslim audiences. Instead of praising Muhammad as he had done before, Malcolm began telling his listeners that what a man did in his relationships with other people to make their lives better was much more important than what he did in his private life. In other words, just because Muhammad had strayed in his private life, the good he had done should not be forgotten.

What Malcolm wanted more than anything else was a chance to sit down with Elijah Muhammad and discuss these problems with him. Why was he suddenly in disfavor? What about these secretaries' claims? The chance came in mid-1963. Malcolm flew to Phoenix for a meeting with Muhammad.

The meeting turned out even worse than Malcolm had feared possible. Muhammad put his arm around Malcolm's shoulders and told him not to worry about these stories, because all he was doing was fulfilling his destiny. "When you read about David taking another man's wife," Malcolm remembered his saying, "I'm that David. You read about Noah, who got drunk. That's me." As for Malcolm's other concern, his own standing in the movement, Muhammad simply told him not to worry and refused to discuss it further.

Malcolm did not know what to do. Although he was certainly worried about his future, he was more concerned about the survival of the Nation of Islam. Because he felt it was necessary to prepare all the other Ministers for the bombshell that might drop at any moment, he began traveling up and down the East Coast discussing the problem and possible solutions. "If we work together and keep our faith in Allah," he told them, "things will work out. This is Allah's way of testing our faith."

But in his heart he knew there was really only one solution. Something had to be done to direct attention away from Muhammad. Evidently Muslim officials in Chicago were thinking the same thing, and they found the very thing that would attract everyone's attention: the question of what was in Malcolm's mind that made him go from Minister to Minister spreading "lies" about Elijah Muhammad. Malcolm was unable to defend himself against the charge without indicting Muhammad. He was totally boxed in. The only thing that would help him, he realized, would be an event as dramatic as the Hinton case. Malcolm would use it to show his devotion to the movement, and the officials needed it so that an excuse might be found to deal with Malcolm X once and for all. The event that occurred was something no one had bargained for.

What happened was one of the most tragic events in American history. On a bright, sunny, cool morning in Dallas, Texas. America's young President, John F. Kennedy, was assassinated, sending the entire nation into shock. Muhammad told all his Ministers that the murder was not to be mentioned in any public speech. But he also asked Malcolm to step in and substitute for him at a speaking engagement in New York City he had scheduled but would not be able to attend. Malcolm agreed to speak. It was to prove a serious mistake.

At the end of his address to the mainly Muslim audience, Malcolm opened the floor to questions. The first question was, as expected, "What do you think about the assassination of President Kennedy? What is your opinion?"

There was a pause as Malcolm gathered his thoughts. "It seems to me that this is just a simple case of chickens coming home to roost." The audience cheered and laughed as Malcolm X added, "Being an old farm boy myself, chickens coming home to roost never did make me sad; they've always made me glad."

This was a direct insult to a nation overcome with grief. When Malcolm realized the terrible reaction his comments would stir he tried to explain his reasoning. The death should not have surprised anyone, he told reporters; it was caused by a national climate of hate. But the press did not accept this explanation. They remembered his comments of a year earlier when a plane carrying 121 white citizens of Atlanta, Georgia, had crashed and burned in France. "I got a wire from God today," Malcolm had gleefully commented. "Somebody came and told me he had really answered our prayers over in France. He had dropped an airplane out of the sky with over 120 white people on it . . . we will continue to pray and hope that every day another plane falls out of the sky!" The reaction of the press, which ran Malcolm's comments in big headlines, was just the ammunition his enemies among the Muslims needed.

Within a week Malcolm was summoned to Phoenix. From the cold reception he received at the airport he knew something big was about to happen. He didn't have to wait long to find out what it was. "You know, Malcolm," said Muhammad, "that was a very bad thing to say. The country loved this man. The whole country is in mourning. That was very ill-timed. A statement like this can make it hard on Muslims in general." He stopped there, took a deep breath and continued, "Malcolm, I'll have to silence you for the next ninety days—so that Muslims everywhere can be dissociated from the blunder."

Muhammad then issued a statement to the press that said, "Malcolm is still a Muslim Minister, but he will not be permitted to speak in public. I have punished him because he has not followed the way of Islam."

Malcolm was shocked. As he was later to say, "I

felt as though something in nature had failed, like the sun or the stars. It was that incredible a thing to me— something too unbelievable to conceive." But there was nothing he could do but accept the suspension. When reporters reached him he told them, "I disobeyed Mr. Muhammad. I must submit completely to his wisdom. I expect to be speaking again after ninety days."

Again, Malcolm was to be proven wrong. He found that the ban was total. Not only was he not to speak to writers and reporters, but he was not even permitted to continue teaching at New York Mosque Number Seven. And behind the scenes more dangerous words were being spoken. High Muslim officials were telling members of the movement, "For the good of the Nation of Islam, Minister Malcolm X really should not be left living." As Malcolm himself knew, there was only one man who would permit words like these to be spoken between Muslims: Elijah Muhammad himself.

What could he do? For the past twelve years he had been able to solve his problems by turning to his faith in Muhammad and the Muslims, and now that was the one place he could not turn. The most important thing, he realized, was to get away from New York, to get some time to sort out his thoughts. He headed toward Miami Beach, Florida, where heavyweight boxer Cassius Clay was in training. Clay, who was later to join the Muslims and change his name to Muhammad Ali, was training to fight another black man, Charles "Sonny" Liston, for the heavyweight championship of the world. This was the first vacation Malcolm had ever taken with Betty, and when Clay pulled one of the greatest upsets in boxing history and defeated Liston it turned out to be an almost perfect stay in Florida. Almost perfect, rather than absolutely perfect, because during these weeks it became obvious to Malcolm that he would never be permitted to rejoin the Nation of Islam. He had become a marked man.

In all his years with the Muslims and even before, during his days as a street hustler, he had been aware that he might be a target for sudden, violent death. It had never really scared him and he had never run from the possibility. Now it was an open secret that the Muslim leadership wanted him dead. A member of Mosque Seven came to Malcolm and told him that he had been asked by one of the Temple's leaders to wire a bomb to the engine of Malcolm's car. The Brother told Malcolm that he just couldn't do it and didn't understand why the leadership wanted to do away with Malcolm X. He could hardly believe the answer Malcolm gave him; indeed, very few Muslims were aware of Muhammad's supposed misdeeds.

It was at this point that Malcolm told writer Alex Haley, who was working with Malcolm on *The Autobiography of Malcolm X,* "I do not expect to live long enough to read my book." He knew how capable the people hunting him were; after all, he himself had trained many of them.

But he was not dead yet, and the problem remained. What should he do? What steps should he take to protect himself and his family? And what about the people who still believed in what he said? Should he just abandon them?

Malcolm counted his assets. First, he had a world-wide reputation. Anything he said would be carried by hundreds of newspapers and reported by most radio and television stations. Second, he had a large non-Muslim following, people who believed what he said but were not willing to follow the harsh code of the Nation of Islam. But what to do with these assets? Malcolm stopped and asked himself what he really offered to the black man, what he had really accomplished over the past twelve years. He began to realize, for the first time, that his contribution might not have been as great as he thought it was.

There was no doubt that he had established himself as an important black leader. The press had called him "the only black man in America who can stop a riot— or start one!" And he knew he was also the only black leader who could talk with both the law students at Harvard and the dope pushers of Harlem. He understood both languages. Finally, after much thought and discussion with close friends and followers, he knew there was only one solution. If he was ever really to help the black man he had to form his own organization. But where would this new movement differ from the Nation of Islam? In conversations late in 1963 Malcolm told famed black writer Louis Lomax, "The messenger has seen God. He was with Allah and was given patience by the Devil. Well, sir, the rest of us Black Muslims have not seen God. The younger Black Muslims want to see some action."

Action! That was where Malcolm's new organization would differ from Muhammad and the Muslims. Malcolm and his followers would get things done—for the entire community of black people. "It will embrace the faith of all black men," Malcolm said in explaining his new organization, "and it will carry into practice what the Nation of Islam only preached."

"Malcolm is forming." The word spread. Many of

the younger Muslims, unhappy with the lack of visible progress the movement had made, let Malcolm know they were ready to join him as soon as he gave the word. To Malcolm's amazement, even white people wrote asking to join his new group. He told them they couldn't become members but their contributions would certainly be appreciated.

It was at this point that Malcolm was to make another of those major changes that marked his life. As a Black Muslim leader he had totally rejected American society, even going as far as to say he no longer considered himself an American. Now he was taking a giant step, moving from just rejecting American society to doing something positive to change it. "I am going to organize and head a new mosque in New York City known as the Muslim Mosque, Incorporated," he told reporters at a large press conference. "This will give us a religious base and the spiritual force necessary to rid our people of the vices that destroy the moral fiber of the community.

"Muslim Mosque, Incorporated will be a working base for an action program designed to eliminate the political persecution, the economic exploitation and the social evils suffered daily by the twenty-two million Afro-Americans."

It all sounded so easy, but Malcolm knew that before his movement got off the ground there would be many problems to face. He knew that his short speech would make the Muslims even more angry then they were and put his life in even more danger. Muhammad had never officially announced that Malcolm was being thrown out of the movement, and most Muslims, not aware of the problems under the surface, would think

Malcolm was leaving the Muslims on his own. And since many of the young Muslims had already pledged to join him, Malcolm's movement could do nothing but harm to the Nation of Islam. A column in *Muhammad Speaks* made the feelings of the Muslim leaders very clear. "Only those who wish to be led to hell," it said, "or to their doom, will follow Malcolm. The die is set and Malcolm shall not escape." The word was thus given—Malcolm X must be destroyed!

Malcolm now became as careful as time allowed. He was constantly looking over his shoulder to see if he was being followed, but the task of setting up his new organization occupied most of his attention.

But even before the long process of getting Muslim Mosque, Inc. established was started Malcolm knew there was one thing he had to do. At least once in his lifetime, every orthodox Muslim must, if at all able, make a trip, or "pilgrimage," to the holy city of Mecca. Mecca, a city in Saudi Arabia, is the birthplace of the original Prophet Muhammad. This pilgrimage to Mecca is known as Hajj. Often during Malcolm's college lectures foreign students, mainly from the Middle East or Asia, would come up to him and say, "You must go to Mecca. You must discover the true Islam." Malcolm realized that they were right, but how could he afford to go? He had been very careful with his money, but with a wife and now two children he had been able to save very little.

Malcolm turned to the same person he had depended on so long ago; he went to Boston to speak to Ella. Ella had never really been a good Muslim. Her independent ways had gotten her suspended from the Boston Temple, and after being reinstated she had decided that the Nation of Islam wasn't really for her and quit. But the Muslim religion fascinated her, and she had been studying under orthodox Muslims living in Boston. She had even gone so far as to found a school where Arabic was taught. As always, she welcomed Malcolm with open arms.

"I want to borrow some money," he told her, "so I can go to Mecca."

Ella didn't even take the time to consider the request. She was quite proud of what Malcolm had become. He had come a long way since those hard days in Michigan so long ago. And although she was saving so that she herself might make the pilgrimage, she knew it would be a more valuable experience for Malcolm. "Whatever I have is yours," she told him.

Malcolm Little, Big Red, Detroit Red, Satan and Malcolm X. As this man of so many different facets made preparations for the longest trip of his life, others were already awaiting his return and plotting his death. But before the enemies met, Malcolm would add another name to his long list of identities.

ten | *The Long Journey Home*

ALTHOUGH Malcolm's connections with the Muslims were broken, his personal views had not really changed. In fact, to his way of thinking, he had not really left the Muslims. He still firmly believed the facts of life as taught to him by Elijah Muhammad: the black man represents all that is good and the white man represents evil.

His opinion of the best solution to the "American problem" had not changed. As he said when announcing the formation of his new group, "I myself intend to be very active in the American Negro's struggle for human rights. I still believe that Mr. Muhammad's analysis of the problem is the most realistic and that his solution is the best one. This means that I too believe the best solution is separation, with our people going back home to our own African homeland." Within a month of making this statement Malcolm was on an airplane, heading toward Cairo, Egypt, the Hajj, and his "African homeland."

The scene that greeted Malcolm at Cairo Airport amazed him. Hundreds and hundreds of Muslims, Muslims of all colors, were greeting each other as if they were long-lost brothers and sisters. Malcolm had never seen whites treating blacks like this, and he wasn't sure he quite understood what was happening. But he was no exception. Although Malcolm was the first "Muslim from America" that these Muslims had ever seen, he was treated as warmly as everyone else. Except for Malcolm, none of the other travelers seemed to notice the difference in skin colors.

As Malcolm later learned, this group was the largest ever to make the Hajj. In Cairo the "pilgrims" took their first step. All the various national styles of dress were exchanged for two simple white towels (one folded around the middle of the body, the other thrown over the left shoulder and back), a pair of simple sandals, and two carrying bags. With everyone dressed the same, all traces of national origin disappeared.

From Cairo the next stop was Jedda, in Saudi Arabia. With growing nervousness Malcolm learned that Jedda was only forty miles from Mecca, but for a while it looked as if those were forty miles he would never travel. After he had handed his passport to custom officials in Jedda, Malcolm was stopped and taken out of line. Because he was from America, he was told, he could not go on to Mecca until he appeared before the Muslim high court. It was the job of the court to make sure that only true Muslims entered Mecca. There was nothing Malcolm could do but wait for the court to convene.

Unfortunately, as he discovered, the court would not be meeting for at least twenty-four hours. He had arrived in Jedda on Friday, a Muslim holy day. Customs officials took him to a large building just outside the airport. He would spend the day there while waiting for the court to meet. It was beginning to look as if he would never find the true Islam.

The "hotel" was filled with people in the same situation as his, people who had come from all over the world to make the Hajj but had been halted at customs. Malcolm was surprised at the vast number of different lands and languages represented. There were Russians and Japanese; there were people from Ghana, Indonesia, Morocco, Egypt, and Korea; and, of course, there was Malcolm X from the United States of America.

Malcolm was brought to a room that he was to share with about fifteen other people. Each individual had his own little section of the room, clearly outlined by the prayer rugs spread all over the room. Malcolm joined them in prayer as best he could. He was embarrassed when he realized how little of the Muslim religion he knew. "Imagine," he said to himself, "being a Muslim Minister, a leader in Elijah Muhammad's Nation of Islam, and not knowing the prayer ritual." The message was clear: The religion he was observing here in Jedda had little connection with the religion he had practiced in America.

The hours seemed endless. After morning prayers,

Malcolm had the honor of being invited to share tea and cookies with a Muslim from the Middle East. He spent the rest of the day exploring the area around the building and waiting for someone to tell him what was going to happen.

Toward the end of the afternoon he remembered something very important. He was not as alone as he thought! Before he left New York he had visited a Muslim official who gave him an official letter of introduction, plus the telephone number of a man in Jedda who spoke English and could offer Malcolm help if he needed it. He certainly did need it.

Malcolm ran down the four flights of steps in the building and found a telephone. Dr. Omar Azzan came right to the airport.

Dr. Azzam was a Swiss-trained engineer who was in Arabia supervising reconstruction work being done on religious structures. More important, from Malcolm's viewpoint, Dr. Azzam's sister was the daughter-in-law of the ruler of Saudi Arabia! All of a sudden everything had turned right for Malcolm. As soon as he arrived at the hotel, Dr. Azzam made a few phone calls and gained permission for Malcolm to go home with him. Malcolm knew his faith in Allah had been rewarded.

When the pair arrived at Dr. Azzam's home his father, Dr. Abd ir-Rahman Azzam, one of Arabia's most distinguished statesman, was waiting. The elder Dr. Azzam had followed Malcolm's career in America with great interest and was extremely happy to meet the "famed" Malcolm X in person. The two spent the rest of the day and a good part of the night discussing the American version of Islam and Malcolm's recent discoveries. When the evening ended Dr. Azzam insisted that Malcolm stay in his spacious room in the Kedda Palace Hotel. In the few hours left that night, Malcolm lay on the big bed and did some serious thinking. As he described it in his autobiography:

"That Dr. Azzam, who was so light-colored he would have been considered a white man in America, with nothing in the world to gain, had given up his room to me for my overnight comfort. He had nothing to gain. He didn't need me. He had everything. In fact, he had more to lose than gain. He had followed the American press about me. He knew what a terrible person I was supposed to be. I was a racist. I was anti-white—and from all appearances he was white. I was supposed to be a criminal; not only that, but everyone was even accusing me of using his religion of Islam as a cloak for my criminal practices and thoughts. Even if he had had some motive to use me, he knew that I was separated from Elijah Muhammad and the Nation of Islam, my power base according to the press in America. I had no job. I had no money. That morning was when I first began to reappraise the white man!" Malcolm was finally beginning to realize that no man can be judged by the color of his skin.

He was finally brought before the High Court on Saturday morning. The Judge asked Malcolm a few questions concerning his reasons for converting to the Muslim religion and making the Hajj. Malcolm's answers satisfied him enough to grant permission for him to make the pilgrimage as well as sign his name in the Holy Register of true Muslims.

"I sincerely hope," the Judge told him, "that when you return to your country you will be a great preacher of the true Islam." Malcolm was on his way to Mecca!

Sitting in a car on the way to Mecca, Malcolm

reflected that he had spent the last fifteen years of his life entering new cities, and yet the excitement never seemed to dull. But as he drove through Mecca he knew he was in the midst of a very different kind of city, a totally new experience. While other cities had impressed Malcolm with their size or their fast pace, it was the calm of Mecca that was overwhelming. The city reminded him of an ancient but extremely proud warrior. It was a monument to the strength of faith, having stood the tests of time and the challenges of an ever-changing world. He felt as if he had been in Mecca all his life and would remain there forever. Malcolm felt as if he had come home.

Many different activities are required of the pilgrim to complete the Hajj. He must circle seven times around a building called the Kaaba, drink from the well of the Zem Zem, run seven times back and forth between the hills of Mt. Al-Safa and Al-Marwah, and recite special prayers in the ancient city of Mina and on Mt. Arafat. Malcolm completed the rituals within a few days. He had made the Hajj.

Then he sat down in his hotel, a piece of paper in front of him, and tried to explain his feelings in a letter to his friends and family in America. But how could he do that when he himself was not sure of his feelings? He had seen many things on his journey that he would have called amazing or unbelievable, but one thing above all others continued to stand out—the total absence of any racial distinction. All his fellow travelers were Muslims —the yellow, the red, the white, and the black—the Europeans, the Asians, the Africans and the American. How could he really explain this in a letter? After many hours of deep thought, this is what he wrote:

"Never have I witnessed such sincere hospitality and

---

the overwhelming spirit of true brotherhood as is practiced by people of all colors and races here in the Holy Land . . . I have been utterly speechless and spellbound by the graciousness I see displayed all around me by people of all colors.

"You may be shocked to hear these words coming from me . . . but what I have seen has forced me to rearrange some of my thought patterns previously held, and to toss aside some of my previous conclusions. I have always kept an open mind, which is necessary in the search for truth. As racism leads America up the suicide path, I do believe, from the experiences that I have had with them, that the whites of the younger generation, in the colleges and universities, will see the handwriting on the wall and many of them will turn to the spiritual path of truth." And he signed the letter with his new Muslim name, "El-Hajj Malik El Shabazz."

Malcolm did not leave Mecca immediately after completing the Hajj. Prince Faisal, the ruler of Saudi Arabia, made him a guest of the state, and he was given use of a chauffeured car and guide. Malcolm spent days touring the city, seeing the brand-new sections of Mecca as well as the ancient religious sections. Along the way Malcolm himself, "The Muslim from America," had become a local attraction. Wherever he went people would stop and ask, through an interpreter, all sorts of questions about America. Malcolm had not changed so much that he could pass up an opportunity to convey his message.

"If you were in America," he told the dark-skinned ones, "you would be called a Negro. There are certain rights you would not have, certain places you couldn't go, places you would not be allowed to eat, drink or even walk inside. You would be pushed and prodded and, possibly, even murdered. All because your skin is black."

Although he hoped his message was getting through to these people, Malcolm was receiving their message. "Your people are not alone," their voices and faces said. He promised himself he would bring this message home to his American brothers and sisters. He would tell them that a majority of the world's population is nonwhite, and that they are all brothers.

Finally, after a visit with Prince Faisal, Malcolm left Mecca. But his trip was far from over. From Arabia he went to Beirut, Lebanon, where he lectured at the University of Beirut. The next stop was the African nation of Nigeria. Speaking at a university there, Malcolm suggested that the future of American blacks was dependent on cooperation with black people all over the world. Thus was born the name of the movement he had simply called Muslim Mosque, Inc. It would be known as The Organization of Afro-American Unity.

In Nigeria, Malcolm was given still another name, this one as an honorary member of the Nigerian Students Society. The name, Omowale, means "the son who has come home." And on this journey that is exactly how Malcolm felt. But when he finally did arrive home, he realized that he had been one of the few granted the opportunity to go to this "homeland" and that if the plight of the black man was to change, the black man had to deal with reality. Reality, in the case of the Afro-American, meant realizing that his future life will be in the United States.

From Nigeria Malcolm went to Ghana, one of the first independent black nations. He was made most welcome there. Newspapers proclaimed his arrival in big headlines, and he was called "the most influential black leader to visit Ghana since W. E. DuBois came here to live."

It was in Ghana that Malcolm had an opportunity to catch up with what was happening in America. What he heard did not make him happy. Almost any violent crime committed in any black ghetto was immediately blamed on "followers" or "sympathizers" of Malcolm X. Secondly, the Muslims had gone to court to have Malcolm, Betty, and their three children thrown out of their home in Queens, New York, a house the Nation of Islam had actually paid for. And finally he learned that American newspapers had reported that a riot had taken place after he spoke in Beirut. There was nothing he could say about this final point; there had been no riot.

Malcolm received many honors in Ghana; he was asked to address the Ghanaian Parliament, and he made speeches to the people and finally was granted an audience with Ghana's famed leader Dr. Kwame Nkrumah. The rest of Malcolm's tour was a whirlwind of invitations, parties, speeches, meetings, awards, honors and plane trips. Before returning to the United States he stopped briefly in Senegal, Liberia, Morocco and Algeria. Finally, two days after his thirty-ninth birthday, he landed in New York.

The year 1964 marked the beginning of a new phase of the black movement. The Senate passed the most far-reaching civil rights bill in history (aside from the Bill of Rights itself) and President Lyndon Johnson signed it into law. But it began to seem that the bill was too little—and too late. The movement had finally turned to violence.

In Harlem, a policeman shot a 15-year-old boy,

and the ghetto erupted into the first of the dreadful "summer riots" that marked the 1960s. In the Harlem riot one person was killed, 140 were injured and 500 were arrested before the police could restore order. No one would even attempt to estimate the damage in terms of dollars and cents.

Other riots followed, in Rochester, New York; Jersey City and Paterson, New Jersey; Philadelphia, and many other cities. Within the next few years few major cities in the nation were left unscarred by racial riots. In 1967, in Detroit, Michigan, 43 people were killed, 2,000 were injured, 1,250 fires were set, and 7,200 people were arrested in one of the biggest riots. Two years earlier, the "Battle of Watts" (34 killed, 1,032 injured, 4,000 arrested) had ravaged part of the city of Los Angeles.

The situation was tailor-made for Malcolm to return and take his place at the head of the new militant black movement. But Malcolm had changed. Instead of calling the riots another example of "chickens coming home to roost" he spoke of working with the established system. The largest gathering of reporters and radio and television newsmen he had ever faced greeted Malcolm at the airport on his return from Mecca. He told them of his new plan. He hoped to organize the black man and take his case to the United Nations. If the United States would not give the black man his rights, Malcolm said, than this country should be brought before the U.N. and denounced. Then a reporter asked Malcolm if, after visiting Africa, he still felt that that was the best place for American blacks.

"No," he answered in a quiet voice, "we must stay here and fight for what is rightfully ours!" And then, before anyone could ask another question, he summed up how he had changed. "In the past," he said, "I have made sweeping indictments of all the white people. I will never be guilty of that again, as I know now that some white people are truly sincere, that some are truly capable of being brotherly toward a black man."

Malcolm quickly moved back into the mainstream of the movement. Once again he followed a maddening schedule of speeches and visits, trying between engagements to get his own movement off the ground. But his major problem had not changed. Those who wanted to follow him were still not sure where he stood. "What do you stand for?" "What do you stand against?"

Even if Malcolm had really known the answer, it would have been hard to explain it. The best he could come up with was, "I'm for truth, no matter who tells it; I'm for justice, no matter who it is for or against. I'm a human being first and foremost, and as such I'm for whoever benefits humanity as a whole."

But he made a point of making sure no one mistook his new stance for weakness. "We still believe that bloodshed is a two-way street, that dying is a two-way street, that killing is a two-way street. I believe in the brotherhood of all men, but I simply do not believe in wasting brotherhood on anyone who doesn't want to practice it with me."

By the time the 1964 Presidential elections rolled around, his change had almost been total. Although he said he would never vote for either of the candidates, Democrat Lyndon Johnson or Republican Barry Goldwater, he urged other blacks to get out and vote. He told an audience at the Harvard Law School, "A large black vote would change the foreign policy as well as the domestic policy of this government. When the black man controls the politics and politicians of his own community, he can make them produce what is good for the community. Once the political control of the so-called Negro community is in the hands of the so-called Negro, then it is possible for us to do something toward correcting the evils and ills that exist there!"

There had indeed been a deep and profound change in Malcolm. He had managed to rise above his position as an American Black Muslim leader and become a symbol to black people all over the world. His thinking now went far beyond the plight of the American black man, and he began using the term "the nonwhites of the world." During a second trip to the middle East in 1965 he met with almost every major leader from that area of the world, from President Nasser of Egypt to President Jomo Kenyatta of Kenya. The trip achieved the same success as his first, and he continued to emerge as an international black leader.

Malcolm returned from his second trip ready to state his position. He knew now what the true goal of his Organization of Afro-American Unity would be: the creation of a society in which blacks and whites lived together in harmony. His change in attitude was the focal point of his OAAU recruitment speeches. "I have seen blacks and whites living together in peace," he told all who would listen, "and so I know it is possible." But even he didn't know when this would happen in America.

He did know his chances of living to see it happen were decreasing rapidly. He never forgot for a moment that there were people constantly searching for him, people trying to find him unprotected for just a moment, waiting for him to make that fatal slip. He knew it would happen. It was now simply a matter of time and place. Yet there was still so much that had to be done. And just not enough time.

eleven | *A Time for Martyrs*

MALCOLM had been through many bleak periods in his life but had always been confident that things would soon be better. Now he was not so sure. He was disturbed by three major problems: trying to get the OAAU off the ground and established, maintaining a constant watch against those who were out to destroy him, and, for the first time in many years, money. On top of all this he was living in constant fear that his enemies would attempt to get at him through his family.

He kept hammering away at these problems, but there just never seemed to be enough hours in the day. The money was, for him, most important because he was supporting Betty and his four daughters. In the past there had always been enough. Malcolm had had his small Muslim expense account, and the Nation of Islam had taken care of most of his family expenses. But that had all changed the day Malcolm left the movement. What little the family had saved went to pay for the two trips to the Middle East, and now, with death at any moment a real possibility, Malcolm was doing his best to provide for the future of his family. There were really only a few ways he could make money. He accepted speaking engagements all over the country, as much for the money as for the chance to get his viewpoint across. And he asked Alex Haley to make sure that all receipts from the book they were writing went to his family and the new movement rather than to the Nation of Islam, for which they had originally been intended.

As for Malcolm's relations with the Black Muslims, they were worse than ever. The Muslims had taken Malcolm to court to force the family to leave the house in Queens, and Malcolm was well aware that it was only a matter of time before the courts ruled for the Muslims.

As for the OAAU, Malcolm's basic problem remained the same. Until he decided on some specific plans and goals, the movement would never succeed. And, as he himself said at this point, "I'm man enough at this moment to tell you that I can't put my finger on exactly how I feel about everything, but I am flexible."

Malcolm had turned out to be a victim of his own popularity. When he had spoken in earlier years, more often than not he was addressing a roomful of people and representing an organization with very specific, outlined goals. Such was no longer the case. When he spoke now, black people all over the world listened. And when he spoke to white people it was as the representative of a vast number of blacks from all over the world, even though in his own mind he was not sure what this great mass of humanity really wanted. He recognized the problem, saying, "What I'm saying now is for myself. Before, it was for and by the guidance of Elijah Muhammad."

And, above all, the death threats continued to reach him. He armed Betty with a shotgun and told her to use it if anyone tried to force his way into the house. He himself made plans to apply for a permit to carry a pistol. But even with these and other precautions the threats soon became actual attempts on his life.

Malcolm was scheduled to speak in Boston, but a conflict in his schedule forced him to send a representative instead. After the speech his representative climbed into a car and headed toward the airport. Halfway there, the car was blocked in the middle of a tunnel. A group of men, supposedly carrying knives, ran from the car that was causing the blockade toward the car carrying the speaker. They were scared away when one of Malcolm's men showed a shotgun that had been hidden in the back seat.

Again, when Malcolm was speaking in Chicago, two cars, both packed with men Malcolm knew from his Black Muslim days, began trailing the car he was riding in. Finally, on a long, straight stretch of road the two trailing cars picked up speed and drew alongside. Thinking quickly, Malcolm picked up a walking cane one of his companions was carrying and stuck it out the side window. The two cars fell back, and Malcolm's car raced to the airport and police protection. But his pursuers were not upset that Malcolm had escaped. They knew they would have other chances.

Malcolm's closest call came on a freezing winter's

night in February, 1965. Malcolm, Betty and their four daughters were asleep in the house in Queens. Suddenly the quiet of the night was shattered by a blast. The house was being fire-bombed! Screaming orders at Betty and gathering the children, he somehow got his family safely from the house. But by the time firemen arrived to extinguish the blaze, the damage had been done. The house had been more than half destroyed. Rebuilding was almost out of the question. Malcolm just had never had enough money to purchase fire insurance.

As he stood there in that cold night watching his home burn, Malcolm thought back through the long years. He realized that he had been through the whole thing before, during his early childhood in Michigan when night riders of another era had burned his father's home.

The Nation of Islam immediately denied having anything to do with the bombing. In fact, James X, who was now serving in Malcolm's old post as Minister of Muslim Mosque Number Seven, told the press he believed Malcolm had placed the bombs himself in order to get favorable publicity.

When he heard that, Malcolm was outraged. "I'm not worried about myself," he told reporters, "But they had better not harm my family. There are the hunters; there are also those who hunt the hunters!"

Those words were probably the harshest he had spoken since his return from Mecca. Those close to him realized that they were seeing a new, calm Malcolm, one quite different from any they had seen before. Famed black writer-photographer Gordon Parks, doing a story on Malcolm for *Life* Magazine, asked Malcolm how he remembered his Muslim days.

As usual, Malcolm thought quite a while before

answering. Finally he said, "That was a bad scene, brother. The sickness and madness of those days—I am so glad to be free of them. It's a time for martyrs now. And if I'm to be one, it will be in the cause of brotherhood. That's the only thing that can save this country. I've learned that the hard way, but I have learned it."

Of course this was a side of Malcolm that would be seen only by the few people close to him—people like Parks, Haley, and Malcolm's wife, Betty. His public image, though toned-down, remained hard. There was no chink in his public armor. For example, at one of the many OAAU organizational meetings in Harlem, an elderly black man, clearly wishing to join Malcolm if he only could understand him, asked the basic question, "We hear you changed, Malcolm. Just where you at with them white folks?"

"I haven't changed," Malcolm answered, "I just see things on a broader scale. For example, I know now that it is smarter to say you're going to shoot a man for what he is doing to you rather than because he is white. If you attack him because he is white you give him an out. He can't stop being white. We've got to give the man a chance. He probably won't take it, the snake. But we've got to give him the chance.

"Now, I don't care what a person looks like or where they come from. My mind is open to anybody who will help get the ape off our backs. That's where I stand." The elderly black man sat down, still not sure just how Malcolm felt about the "devil" white man.

As the winter days grew shorter, Malcolm's schedule grew longer. He flew to Selma, Alabama, to address a civil rights rally and was warned by black leaders there not to say anything in favor of violence. From there he flew to France, where he was scheduled to address an African student group. But when he landed in Paris he found that the French government had branded him an "undesirable person." Not only was he not allowed to speak, but he would never be permitted to enter France again!

Malcolm objected mildly, but there was little he could do. There were more pressing problems at home. Since the bombing, his family had been staying with close friends while they searched for a suitable house. A court order had finally been issued ordering the family to vacate the house in Queens.

Scant days after the order was issued, Malcolm took the last of his undamaged possessions from the half-destroyed house. He sadly looked over the few things his family could actually call their own. It was a pitifully small pile. Malcolm realized then how little, in terms of material things, he had given his family. It occurred to him that he had never given any of his daughters a real surprise, and as for Betty—well, it was a major disappointment for him when he realized how often he had left her alone and traveled across the nation. In the future, he vowed, he would never travel anywhere without her. If there was a future. . . .

There was not much more of one. On February 18, 1965, Malcolm spoke to a capacity crowd in the Barnard Gymnasium at Columbia University. It was to be his last formal address. "We are living in an era of revolution," he began, "and the revolt of the American Negro is part of that rebellion. It is incorrect to classify the revolt of the Negro as simply a racial conflict of black against white, or as a purely American problem. Rather, we are today seeing a global rebellion of slaves against slave-owners, the ones who are being taken advantage of against those who take advantage.

"The Negro revolution is not a racial revolt. We are interested in practicing brotherhood with anyone really interested in living according to it. But the white man has long preached an empty doctrine of brotherhood which seems little more than the Negro accepting his status as a second-class citizen in society." Malcolm, as was usual in these days, was cheered by the almost all-white audience.

Malcolm spent most of the following day with Gordon Parks. The two sat for many hours trying to figure out exactly what role Malcolm had played thus far in the black struggle. Parks then asked Malcolm if those stories he had been hearing about Malcolm's being marked for death were true. "It's as true as we're sitting here. They've tried it twice in the past two weeks."

When Parks suggested that he get police protection, Malcolm gave his familiar chuckle and said, "Brother, nobody can protect you from a Muslim but another Muslim—or an individual trained in their tactics. I know; I invented many of them." At the end of the day, Malcolm and Gordon said goodbye . . . for the last time.

Saturday had been reserved for house-hunting with Betty. Although he still owed Ella more than a thousand dollars, Malcolm was sure that the publisher of his autobiography would advance him enough money to make a down payment on a place to live. But finding a house was not that easy. There were many neighborhoods not open to Malcolm because of his black skin. Even some integrated neighborhoods were closed because the blacks who lived there were afraid. They had integrated peacefully and didn't want Malcolm coming in and "rocking the boat." Malcolm had to smile bitterly at these black men who had forgotten their heritage. It didn't make him angry, just sorry for them.

But finally a real estate man did find something in a predominantly white, Jewish neighborhood on Long Island. Both Malcolm and Betty agreed it would be just perfect for them. Malcolm told the broker he would let him know Monday morning, as soon as he had spoken to his publisher. When Monday morning arrived, Betty had forgotten all about the house. She was busy making plans for her husband's funeral.

Malcolm and Betty separated late Saturday afternoon. He drove into the city and checked into the New York Hilton Hotel, planning to spend the night preparing the speech he was scheduled to give the following afternoon. As he checked into the hotel he realized that, for the first time he could remember, he was almost afraid to go into Harlem. Here he was checking into a downtown hotel, an exile from the black people of Harlem. Although Black Muslims were seen around the hotel, Malcolm spent an uneventful night.

Sunday morning he did something quite unusual. He called Betty and asked her to dress the children and bring them to the Audubon Ballroom to hear his speech that afternoon. Although less than twenty-four hours earlier he had requested that they stay away, Betty readily promised to be there. "Goodbye," Betty said finally.

"Yes," Malcolm answered, "goodbye."

"Asalaikum, brothers and sisters!" said the tall, proud, bearded black man.

"Asalaikum salaam!" came the reply from the audience seconds before the murderous shots rang out, "Peace be with you also, brother."

Recently returned from his first trip to the Middle East, Malcolm discusses his new feelings with reporters (1964)

Family, friends, and neighbors attend last rites for the fallen leader

The day after Malcolm's assassination the Muslim mosque in Harlem was burned almost to the ground. The fire is still smoldering as New York City firemen attempt to quell it.

Demanding more Negro representation in the academic community and curriculum, black students seize control of Ford Hall at Brandeis University, January 1969. Dispute was settled without the use of force.

twelve | *Epilogue*

EVEN before the last of his assassins' bullets found their mark, Malcolm X the man was dying and Malcolm X the legend was being born. In the years that have passed, Malcolm has been anything but forgotten. Many books analyzing his life and ideas have been written and published, a documentary movie about his life has been made, a play dealing with the night of the day he died was produced on Broadway, a ballet has been dedicated to him, sculptures have been done, blacks all over America honor his memory on the day he died, and even a small university has been named after him. All these tributes were dedicated as much to the principles of black freedom that he stood for as they were to the man. And, as is natural, others have come along to step into the leadership position he created.

As for his murderers, they were soon brought to justice. Thomas Hagan, Norman 3X Butler and Thomas 15X Johnson were convicted of first-degree murder and sentenced to life imprisonment.

The first of the important memorials to the life of Malcolm X appeared just a few months after his death. The book he and Alex Haley were working on, *The Autobiography of Malcolm X,* was published and ardently received by both blacks and whites. The original publisher, the company that paid Malcolm his advances, almost killed the project. After his death they feared that putting the autobiography into bookstores would lead to violence and decided not to publish it. A second publishing company, Grove Press, stepped in and agreed to print the book. They have been greatly rewarded. *The Autobiography of Malcolm X* went through eighteen printings in less than five years. More than a million copies were sold in that time. Among high school and college students it is endlessly read and discussed. In fact, because so many teachers are using it in their classrooms, Grove Press has issued a study guide to be used with the book. The *Autobiography* has taken its place among American biographical classics and is considered necessary reading by anyone interested in understanding the black movement within the United States.

Politically the legend of Malcolm X is always present. As he sat on the stage in Selma, Alabama, shortly before his death, he leaned over and told Mrs. Martin Luther King how glad he was to be there with her husband. Then he stood up and told the audience, "Whites had better be glad Martin Luther King is rallying the people . . . because other forces are waiting to take over if he fails."

The message was clear. Malcolm had fully accepted his most important place in the movement. He provided the alternative to calm, peaceful, brotherly existence between blacks and whites. The extreme elements of the black movement, those preaching hatred, violence, and separatism, could only succeed if the more moderate branches of the movement failed completely. If you don't accept the olive branch of peace offered to you by people like Dr. King, Malcolm was telling white America, then you'll have to deal with the sword.

The American people were listening. In the elections of 1966 blacks were elected as Mayors in Cleveland, Ohio, and in Flint, Michigan. In Massachusetts, Edward Brooke became the first black man elected to the Senate since just after the Civil War. A year later, blacks were elected Mayor of Gary, Indiana, and of smaller towns, and Thurgood Marshall became the first black man appointed to the Supreme Court of the United States.

But all was not peaceful. Major riots occurred in a great number of cities all across the nation and, on April 4, 1968, Dr. Martin Luther King was assassinated.

An entire new generation of black leaders, using new slogans, has sprung up. "Black Power" first became a rallying cry back in 1966 and has since come to mean "Black voting power," "Black economic power," and "Black social power." Accompanying that call came the oft-used phrase "Black is Beautiful," Afro-haircuts and even a song by black soul-singer James Brown entitled, "Say It Loud, I'm Black And I'm Proud," became a hit.

Malcolm's doctrine of race pride is daily gaining acceptance.

As for the individuals who took his place, the first to step into the void created by Malcolm's death was Stokely Carmichael, who spoke of black separatism. H. Rap Brown, who told America to give blacks their rights or face destruction, followed, as did Eldridge Cleaver and Bobby Seale, all three members of a new black militant group known as the Black Panthers.

Black college professor Harry Edwards moved on a different front. Since Afro-Americans have taken their place at the head of the American sports scene (better than 50 percent of all the professional basketball players in America are black, for example), Edwards attempted to organize a black boycott of the 1968 Olympic Games. In part he succeeded. Two of the blacks who did choose to participate and won their races, John Carlos and Tommie Smith, gained world-wide attention when they stood on the award stand and, as the American National Anthem played, raised their black-glove-covered fists straight up in the air in the "Black Power" salute as a tribute to black people all over the world.

As far as the Nation of Islam is concerned, it is still an important force, though it has faded from the front pages of the newspapers. Late in the 1960s Elijah Muhammad, then in his eighties, announced that the Black Muslims would become more active in economic areas, particularly moving into self-owned farms and businesses. A study made in early 1970 put the value of all Muslim-owned property at $20,000,000.

The role of the Muslims as a rallying point for militant blacks has been taken over by the Black Panthers. The Panthers, headed by people like Seale and

Cleaver, often quote Malcolm X in their philosophy and have succeeded in gaining the support of many blacks. The Panthers are more militant, though, than Malcolm would ever have approved. Malcolm talked about "getting guns," but this was his way of striking fear into the hearts of white people in order to get results. The Panthers have actually gone out and gotten the guns—and the result has been a series of gun battles with police all across the nation, with both sides losing.

Malcolm's new group, the Organization of Afro-American Unity, never really got off the ground after his death, although it was still in existence as late as 1969. Headed by Malcolm's proud half-sister from Boston, Ella Collins, it remained small and struggling, never gaining a membership greater than two hundred.

And so the story of Malcolm X has never really ended. He is truly bigger in death than in life. And as long as someone speaks of pride and independence, dedication and deep feeling, and, most important, freedom, the life of Malcolm X will never be forgotten.